T0054401

YOUR SINGING QUESTIONS ANSWERED

A HANDBOOK FOR BEGINNING SINGERS

JEFF & CRYSTAL DEA MOORE

ISBN 979-8-35092-063-5

To the unsung heroes of everyday life who hold extraordinary dreams. To all who believe that every voice matters and those who yearn to be the finest version of themselves. May this book provide guidance in a world filled with chaos, and your path lead you to the place where your voice soars highest.

TABLE OF CONTENTS

INTRODUCTION

As a beginning singer, do you have questions about how to sing better or what various singing terms mean? Have you ever googled one or more of these questions? If you have, you may have been overwhelmed by the number of results that come up. When you dive in to review recommended websites, how do you know if the information is credible? What do you do with contradictory information? What should you take as fact? What information can really help improve your singing? It's difficult to assess the quality of information when you're a beginner – you don't know what you don't know! If you can relate, this book is for you.

We've done the work of sorting through the Internet garbage for you. In these pages, we've answered the most googled questions asked by beginning singers and provided specific exercises to help you improve your singing which can be found for free at our website: YourSingingQuestionsAnswered. com. Why are our answers better than the ones you may find in a search or even through AI? To put it simply, we have the education, knowledge, and real-life experience that make us experts. We take the most up-to-date evidence about what helps singers improve and combine that with our experience applying it in our studio to give you the most recent, accurate, and targeted information and exercises to help you become the singer you want to be.

Both of us hold professional certificates in music (Jeff in Voice Styles and Master Guitar, and Crystal in Bass) from Berklee College of Music. In addition to his studies at Berklee, Jeff is a certified Master Voice Instructor from the Vocalist Studio and has studied the voice extensively with teachers both domestically and internationally. He is well versed in the science of singing and how technology can be utilized to promote vocalists' growth. Truth be told, Jeff is a singing nerd.

In addition to her musical training, Crystal's background is in higher education and behavioral science, and she knows the best ways to teach people new skills. As a qualified teacher of Mindfulness-Based Stress Reduction (MBSR), she deeply understands the mind-body connection and how great singing is deeply rooted in the management of stress, tension, and positive self-talk.

Together, we make a great team. We're both committed to and passionate about helping people become better singers. Singing increases quality of life, is good for your health, and helps people make positive connections with others. We all should be singing more often!

Not only do we have the education to answer your questions competently and correctly, Jeff has almost a decade of experience working with hundreds of vocalists in our guitar and singing studio in upstate New York. He has taken his education, knowledge, and this in-person teaching experience to produce a method of voice instruction that really works if you are willing to spend 15 minutes a day doing prescribed workouts.

Our students say things like, "Jeff has taken my voice leaps and bounds over where I thought it could be," "Jeff explains why each exercise can improve your voice, and if you listen to the instruction, your singing will be better," "I've been singing a long time but there were still issues with my vocals, and Jeff's instruction solved these issues better than any other voice teacher I've had." These testimonials are a result of the instruction and students' engagement with the assigned exercises 15 minutes a day. We guarantee your voice will improve if you follow our instructions.

In this book, we promise to give you accurate answers (at this writing as singing science is constantly evolving) to common singing questions that are based on real evidence, both scientific and experiential. If you study these answers and do the prescribed exercises 15 minutes a day, we guarantee your singing will improve in 60 days. If you don't see any benefits, we will refund the money you spent on this book!

This book is intended for beginning to intermediate singers who have little formal training and knowledge of music theory but have a passion for singing. Readers can choose to read from beginning to end or jump to various sections in which they are most interested. Any terms that are covered in other chapters that may be unfamiliar to a beginner are bolded and defined in the glossary. At the end of each chapter are the most effective exercises to take your singing to the next level. Our companion website, YourSingingQuestionsAnswered.com, provides free audio files you need to do the exercises plus other helpful resources to help you progress along your singing path.

Don't delay, start reading and doing your workouts NOW! Our students consistently bemoan the fact that they did not start their singing studies earlier. While singing won't solve all your problems, we know it will enrich your life and make it better. And who doesn't need that?

Finally, please feel free to contact us through our website with any comments or questions for either one of us. We always learn so much from other singers, and always welcome messages from our readers. We promise we will answer!

So, keep on singing, keep getting better at it, and let's make the world a better place.

Musically yours,
Jeff and Crystal Moore
August 2023

CHAPTER 1

UNDERSTANDING PITCH MATCHING AND HOW TO GET BETTER AT IT

I n our experience, all singers are concerned about their ability to sing the right notes in songs. Becky, one of our in-person students, has a beautiful, resonant voice, but many of the notes she sings are either sharp or flat, making her performances sound just a little off. This inability to consistently match pitch was what brought Becky to our studio. She commented, "I sound pretty good when I'm singing with the artist, but when I sing to a backing track where I fill in the vocals, something just isn't right."

That something is her ability to match pitch.

At the beginning of her training, she had difficulty identifying which pitches were off and what segments of the song needed the most work. But as she trained in the studio and at home using an online pitch detector, her ear improved, as did her ability to match pitches more consistently. This took time—short but consistent practice sessions coupled with feedback from her singing coach and the app helped Becky become the type of singer she has always wanted to be.

This chapter answers your questions about pitch matching and provides you with the tools you need to improve. Let's get started!

WHAT IS PITCH MATCHING?

Pitch matching is singing the right note. But what's the right note? It's the note that is being played by an instrument or sung by another person. Pitch matching implies that there is a pitch that needs to be mimicked (or matched). For example, it could be a piano note, a guitar note, or a person singing a note. It involves hearing the note and then being able to reproduce it. The person singing needs to determine, by ear, what note needs to be sung. This can be challenging for beginners, but it's a skill that can be learned in a matter of weeks although it can take several months to become proficient. Just like other musical skills, matching pitch is something that you get better at as you progress as a singer. Given how difficult it is at the beginning, it's a skill that frustrates most vocalists because it interferes with you being able to sing the way you would like. This is why it must be addressed as early as possible in your singing journey. Once you have the capability to do this, singing becomes challenging and rewarding rather than frustrating and ego shattering.

WHAT IS PITCH IN MUSIC?

Pitch refers to the frequency of a certain note, which is how fast the sound waves are vibrating. Slow vibrations are low in pitch. Fast vibrations are high notes. For example, middle C (which is an often-cited reference note and is also called C4 on a piano) creates sound waves that vibrate at 256 hertz (Hz) or 256 cycles per second. The note A above middle C vibrates at 440 cycles per second. The higher the note, the faster it vibrates. Most people can hear notes between 50 Hz and 15,000 Hz, with some people able to hear up to 20,000 Hz.

It is helpful to use a piano keyboard to help visualize where various pitches are in relation to one another. See Graphic 1.1. The keys on the left are lower in pitch than the keys on the right.

Graphic 1.1

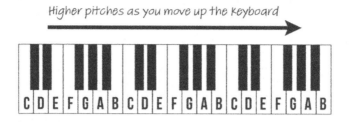

HOW ARE PITCHES OR NOTES NAMED?

Referring to Graphic 1.1, if you play the white keys, starting from middle *C* and going from left to right, this is the sequence of notes: *C, D, E, F, G, A, B*, and then it goes back to *C*. (This is also called the C-major scale, but let's not worry about that now!) You can continue this cycle until you run out of piano keys. As the notes get higher in pitch, it is easy to see that the next *C* will be higher than the previous one. When a cycle ends and the note returns to *C*, that's an octave. It's the same thing with the next octave down, where the pitch is lower. That sequence of notes going to the left would be *C, B, A, G, F, E, D, C*. All notes have octaves.

Sometimes you will see notes with numbers attached to them. For example, *C4* (or *c4*) denotes the *C* note in the fourth octave. *C2* is the *C* note in the second octave, which is two octaves down from *C4*. We refer to a singer's range using this system, which we discuss in Chapter 2.

The black keys on the piano are sharps if you are moving up in pitch, but are flats if you are moving down in pitch. Moving along the piano keys from *C* and playing all the keys, including the black ones, results in this sequence of notes: *C, C♯, D, D♯, E, F, F♯, G, G♯, A, A♯, B*). Moving down in pitch involves flats (same pitches, different names), so the sequence would be *C, B, B♭, A, A♭, G, G♭, F, E, E♭, D, D♭*. Notice that there is no sharp or flat between *E* and *F* and *B* and *C*. You can physically see this on the piano. Here is a keyboard with note names and sharps and flats labeled.

Graphic 1.2

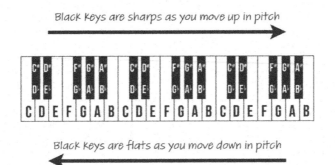

Black keys are sharps as you move up in pitch

Black keys are flats as you move down in pitch

WHAT IS THE DIFFERENCE BETWEEN PITCH AND DYNAMICS?

As discussed above, pitch is the actual frequency of the notes (how fast the sound waves are vibrating). Dynamics refers to how loud the pitch is sung or played. The same note can be soft or loud. As you turn up the volume, it doesn't change the note. And as rockers, we like it loud!

WHAT IS AN OCTAVE?

An octave is the same note at a higher or lower frequency, which means it is vibrating at double or half the frequency. For example, middle C vibrates at 256 Hz, and the C above middle C vibrates at 512 Hz. The C below middle C vibrates at 123 Hz. Another way to think about it is that an octave is the same note, just sung or played higher or lower than the reference note. See Graphic 1.3 to see where these are on the piano. For example, the note of the higher octave for middle C is the next C to the right. The note of next lower octave from middle C is the next C to the left.

Graphic 1.3

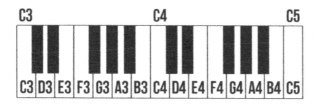

You can also test this with your voice by singing the song that almost everyone knows: Do, Re, Mi, Fa, Sol, La, Ti, Do. Once you hit that second Do, that is the octave. But remember, you've got to work on your pitch matching to make sure you're singing the right note.

IS PITCH MATCHING HARD?

Pitch matching is hard if you've never done it before, but with the right exercises and time, you can do it. The biggest obstacle is how most people approach it. They sing along with their favorite song, sung by the original artist, and this is the slowest way to learn how to match pitch. This gives you a guide tone and is not the way to develop pitch matching. Pitch matching is developed by doing exercises that challenge your ability to match a note.

How long does it take to competently match pitch? That depends on the person and the note. Usually, it's easier to sing notes that are in your speaking range (which is also called **chest voice**). To match pitch relatively well can take from two to six months, depending on age, health, and how often and long you practice during each session. Assume you're working on pitch matching with a visual reference (e.g., online pitch detector) and spending fifteen to twenty minutes a day on it. If you are over the age of sixty and have never sung before, it may take six months to a year to reliably match pitch. On the other hand, if you are in your twenties and sang in the glee club in junior high, it may take you less time than that.

Remember that matching pitch is an ability that doesn't have a top end. You can always enhance your skill set. For example, you've developed good pitch matching, but how long does it take for you to find and lock on to the note? We call that singing metric speed of resolution – how long it takes a singer to lock on to a pitch. That is a skill related to pitch matching that will continue to develop over time.

Assuming you can hear the note (and that means you aren't tone deaf—don't worry, most people aren't), it comes down to positioning your vocal folds correctly. See Graphic 1.4 below for an image of your vocal folds. Positioning vocal folds correctly can be difficult given most people aren't even aware of where they are! To help you to begin to position them correctly, we recommend using a visual aid (e.g., an online pitch detector or app).

Pitch detectors will allow you to sing into the app, and the app will tell you what note you are hitting. This is where it is important for you to pay attention to how your throat feels. What is the sensation when you hit the note correctly? Using a pitch detector and paying attention to your body sensations gives you automatic feedback about how your vocal folds are positioned. When you begin formal training on your pitch matching, you don't want to start too low or too high. If the note is outside of your range, then you can't match it. It's harder to match pitch around your **break** or at the extreme ends of your range than it is in your easy, speaking chest voice.

Graphic 1.4

OPEN AND CLOSED FOLDS/CORDS

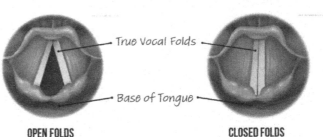

True Vocal Folds

Base of Tongue

OPEN FOLDS   CLOSED FOLDS

HOW DO I KNOW IF I AM SINGING THE RIGHT NOTE?

At the beginning of their singing journey, many vocalists would say that you know you're singing the right notes if your audience doesn't run away from you! This gets to the heart of the matter. Most people can sing and sing well given the right training, but most give up before they develop the ability because the time and effort competent singing requires.

Once you train your ear to hear the appropriate note, you can determine with a very high degree of accuracy if you are singing the intended note. Ear training is using your ear (or aural skills) to identify pitches, melodies, chords, and other musical concepts. Ear training comes with time, and as you study voice more and more, you get better and better at it. It's a skill that is essential for being able to sing the correct note. If you don't know if you're singing the right note, you probably aren't.

Until you can reliably use your ear to determine if you're singing the correct note, use an app to help develop your ear. This will help you develop this skill at a much faster pace than you could without the use of technology. With a pitch detecting app, you've got visual feedback that helps you progress much more quickly.

You also need to know your **range** so you can work on matching pitch within it (in other words, what notes are you currently capable of singing?).Understanding your **chest voice** and **head voice** is also important. Once you determine this, then you know what notes to train with. It doesn't do much good to train with scales that are above or below your range to sing. Think about it. If you aren't physically able to reproduce the note, what good will it do to match these pitches? You'll only frustrate yourself and as you learn to improve your singing, and you certainly want to avoid any unnecessary frustration!

HOW DO I GET BETTER AT MATCHING PITCH?

Matching pitch is like any other skill: to get better, you need to practice it, but the best method is not by singing songs. Why? Because the best way to build your voice is to specifically work on areas that need improvement. Melody lines are made to be easy to sing and intuitive. To hone pitch-matching skills, work on notes in your range that are difficult, such as those that are at the extreme ends or the notes around your **break**. Movement of the notes in songs is important, but songs aren't usually written to challenge your pitch-matching ability.

Competent singing requires the ability to move between notes both slowly and quickly, as well as reaching notes that are both high and low. A goal you may set is the ability to match pitch on every note in your range so that your songs sound awesome. This also implies that you know how your voice responds in different parts of your range. For example, it's usually harder to match pitch at your break than it is to match pitch at the high end of your range. For the beginner or a person having difficulty matching pitch, using a chromatic track to practice pitch matching is the way to go. Chromatic means that you start on a certain note and either go up or down the keyboard, playing every note between that first note and an ending note.

If you look at Graphic 1.2, presented earlier in the chapter, a chromatic track plays both the white and black keys in either ascending or descending order. Depending on the starting or ending note, some notes you'll try to match pitch will be out of your range. Find out which notes are in your range (and yes, you can extend your range, but this is another skill covered in Chapter 2) and understand that, as a beginner, your range will likely be limited. If you are trying to hit those high notes, don't strain! You can damage your voice. Be sure to warmup before you begin by using **lip trills**.

WHAT IS THE BEST EXERCISE FOR LEARNING TO MATCH PITCH?

For most people who have pitch-matching difficulty, the exercise below is the single best exercise to learn to effectively match pitch. Do this exercise for five to ten minutes per day, five days per week. You should begin to see incremental changes in your ability to match pitch in about three weeks. You can use a keyboard, a singing app, or visit our website for resources to support the following exercise. The website also provides a chromatic track to help you match pitch: YourSingingQuestionsAnswered.com.

Sing to a chromatic scale starting at *C2* (that is for lower voices) and *C3* (for higher voices), and go up as high as you can go. With practice, higher voices should be able to get close to *C6*, and lower voices should be able to get to *C5* or close.

CHAPTER 2

LEARNING ABOUT SINGING/ VOCAL RANGES AND HOW TO EXPAND YOURS

G reg is fifty-five years old has been singing since his high school. Greg has anxiety and a habit of singing along with the artist on recordings as his practice routine. When he visited our studio, we tested his pitch matching and range, and found he had a difficult time matching pitch, especially around his **break**. He consistently sings two to three steps lower (i.e., lower notes) than the melody line for most songs when he is singing a karaoke version.

Greg's issues are both psychological and physical. He fears singing a wrong note, so he avoids notes that he thinks may be too high, and this has resulted in him hitting the wrong notes quite a bit. His singing sounds off key to him and others. While his presentation (expression, dynamics) is solid, he lacks one of the basic abilities of singing: Understanding the bounds of his range, which is necessary to effectively train on pitch matching.

Greg was given a chromatic pitch workout (see Chapter 1) with a pitch detector that identifies his pitch so he can get instant feedback about the notes he's hitting. Within a three-month period, Greg corrected many of his issues with pitch and has a good grasp of his range. Over this time, he even extended his usable range by four notes! These workouts, coupled with mindfulness techniques, have reduced his anxiety. With six months of regular workouts, Greg is singing songs that he likes, and they're on pitch! He continues to add notes to his useable range.

WHAT IS SINGING RANGE?

Range is the notes you can sing. This is generally consecutive, chromatic notes, but based on your **break/passaggio** (covered in Chapter 3), there may be notes in the middle of your range that the beginner has difficulty singing. In fact, many beginners think they can't sing high notes because they're actually using the wrong muscle group to sing. Our speaking voice utilizes what most people call chest voice, and this is the range of notes governed by our **TA muscle group** (thyroarytenoid muscle). Don't worry, you don't have to be able to pronounce this, and throughout the book we will refer to this as the TA muscle group. Musculature related to singing is covered in Chapter 3.

WHAT ARE SINGING RANGES CALLED?

In Chapter 1, we learned how notes are named, so if you aren't familiar with the designations (e.g., C4–C6), please revisit Chapter 1. These are the note ranges for classical voice designations:

Table 2.1: Classical Singing Designations

Voice Type	Beginning Note	End Note
Soprano	C4	C6
Alto	F3	E5
Tenor	C3	C5
Baritone	G2	G4
Bass	E2	E4

As you can see, there is overlap in these designations. Graphic 2.1 demonstrates this.

Graphic 2.1

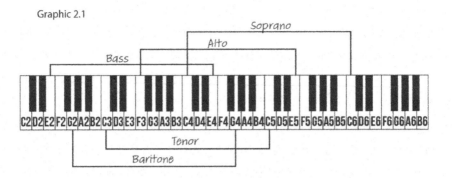

Why are each of the ranges two octaves? Primarily, it's for the convenience of conductors and composers. In our studio, we don't use the classical singing designations, and believe the antiquated system is something contemporary singers should avoid because it can be limiting. While it may be interesting to find out your classification, don't limit yourself to that range. Everyone has a comfortable singing range, but that singing range can be expanded with consistent work. The person with the widest range (Tim Storms) has a reported ten octaves of singing voice and holds the *Guinness World Book of Records* for the lowest note produced by a human. We bet he doesn't care about his classical singing classification!

Here are some questions to help you ponder the classical singing-classification quandary:

1. Why do classical coaches tell singers they must fit into one voice type when it's demonstrated that the average person can train and sing across several of the classical voice designations?

2. Why do classical coaches point to studies indicating that moving out of a classical classification for singing can damage the voice? Note: These studies were generally done in the mid-twentieth century or earlier, before contemporary voice training, and are not based on the latest evidence produced from the latest voice science.

3. Can the average person sing outside of their natural singing range? As we have indicated, the answer is a resounding yes.

With proper voice training and voice care, most people can sing at least three octaves and often can sing four or more. Most of our students (regular people like you) who have been training with us for a while have ranges of four and five octaves, and they can use all of these octaves to sing songs and workouts. Our students are not gifted when it comes to singing and are average when it comes to voice capability. What distinguishes them is their dedication to learning how to expand their useable range. They work steadfastly on their voices and train at least five days per week.

Here is a caveat: It's true that forcing your voice to go to notes that are too high can damage your voice. This is the same for any other activity. An untrained person can easily hurt themselves in a gym or in a running situation. So, as you train to expand your range, be sure to properly **warmup** and take care of your voice. Proper training, not genetics, determines most of your capability when it comes to total range.

WHAT IS THE AVERAGE OR MOST COMMON SINGING RANGE?

For most people (and there are always exceptions) the average singing range is about one to one-and-a-half octaves from about C3 to C4. In our studio, we have tested hundreds of untrained vocalists from six to eighty years of age, and this maxim holds true. We find that children may have problems getting below F3 and above A4 if they haven't trained.

The most common classical singing designation is soprano for women and baritone for men, but this is debatable. Your voice changes over time, especially without training. A woman's voice (untrained) will get deeper as she ages into middle and old age, and a man's voice will deepen through puberty and get higher as he ages. These changes are primarily due to fluctuations in hormones over the life span. With training, your voice will mature and continue to improve over time. If you train your voice regularly and don't smoke, you can expect improvement well into your eighties! Wouldn't it be cool to be rocking the house as an octogenarian? Think about Mick Jagger of the Rolling Stones. Some critics say his voice has improved as he has entered old age.

WHAT ARE THE SINGING RANGES OF SOME FAMOUS SINGERS?

We haven't tested these singing stars in our studio, so are relying on the information that comes from the star's marketing department or is based on pitch-corrected recordings (how high and low they sing on their releases), so this is an estimation. But this does give you an idea about singing ranges and how you can likely match the ranges of some of these superstars!

Table 2.2: Ranges of Famous Singers

Singer	Number of Octaves
Rob Halford	6
Adam Lopez	6
Mariah Carey	5
Paul McCartney	5
Whitney Houston	5
Brendon Urie	4
David Bowie	4
Ariana Grande	4
Christina Aguilera	4
Hayley	4
Freddie Mercury	4
Billie Eilish	3
Janice Joplin	3

WHAT IS THE DIFFERENCE BETWEEN VOCAL RANGE AND VOCAL REGISTERS?

As we've discussed above, your vocal range is the range of pitches you're able to sing—the lowest pitch you can accurately hit to the highest pitch you can sing. Vocal registers have to do with the muscle group that you're using to hit the pitches, which includes **head, chest, and mixed voice**. Vocal register can also refer to the way someone's voice sounds in terms of its resonance or richness. As with the classical classifications, very little of the vocal process has been rigorously and scientifically reviewed and classified. In Chapter 3, we take a deep dive into the realm of vocal registers and bring you the best information from the science of singing vocal science that is backed by our experience with hundreds of students in our studio.

WHAT IS TESSITURA?

Tessitura is your comfortable singing range. This is where you want to sing most of your songs, and one of the reasons why one changes the **key of a song**. The goal of training is to have a broad tessitura so you can comfortably sing songs in several keys.

WHAT IS MY SINGING RANGE?

A word of caution: To find your range, don't do what the majority of singing apps and so-called coaches on the Internet tell you to do—sing as low as you can go and then squeak as high as you can go and . . . ta dah! You've got your range. Wrong! To really understand your range, it needs to be tested with some level of care and rigor.

As a reminder, range is defined as the consecutive notes you can sing chromatically (singing notes up or down the keyboard without skipping any keys). Matching pitch means that you don't stray into an adjacent pitch during the period of matching. We define the period of matching as 1.5 seconds. So, if you can sing *C4* for 1.5 seconds, congratulations! You matched one pitch! And as you get better, the time it takes to match a pitch will decrease. We call the time it takes you to to lock on a pitch is the speed of resolution.

We recommend that beginners test their range two or three times a week using a high-quality singing or pitch-matching app as they learn to match pitch to get feedback on their progress. You can manually test your range by getting a keyboard or other instrument on which you know where *C4* is located. Play the tone, sing the tone. Did you match it? If you have an untrained ear, you might not be able to tell if you can accurately match the pitch, so it is best if you use a quality singing app to test it. Make sure you are matching for at least a couple of seconds; if not, you are likely straining to get to notes because you haven't built up the necessary support musculature that keeps us on pitch.

HOW DO I EXPAND MY SINGING RANGE?

Given your musculature and vocal fold size, training will optimize the notes you're able to sing based on your physiology. How big are your vocal folds? This determines how low you can go. How trained are your muscles? This determines high range. Most people do not specifically train the **CT muscle group**, which is involved in your head voice. They tend to train their **mixed voice**, which allows their head voice to be utilized to some extent. Most people want to train the aspects of the voice that sound more resonant and richer than they want to train the head voice, which can sound thin. Our experience and vocal science evidence indicates that it is vital to train your full range if you want to sing a variety of songs in different styles.

Safely test and push your range (but don't strain your voice!). Lock in the new pitches through daily training. Continue to train. We know this works. Jeff had a high note of *A4* when he started training and was able to work to a usable range of *F5* and an absolute range of *A5*. (Usable range is what you can use in a song. Absolute range is what you can hit when you are trying to match pitch with a keyboard or app.)

Here are the five steps we guarantee will expand your range.

1. Learn to match pitch at a simple level (using a quality app is ideal at this point).

2. Make sure you warmup first! To get you started, use **lip trills** (also called **lip rolls**) or use the vowel *ah*, as in father. Don't force your voice but do test your range.

3. If the highest note you could sing last week was *F♯4*, then try for *G4* this week, but don't yell, shout, or over contract (i.e., tense up and push). If you feel pain or discomfort, stop what you're doing and always make sure you're healthy when you start to seriously train any muscle group. If you have pain or discomfort, consult a doctor!

4. Sing a chromatic run of notes where each note is held for at least for seconds. Use a variety of **singing vowels** while training daily.

5. Test at least twice a week.

HOW DO I SING HIGH NOTES?

As we pointed out earlier, you need to train your CT muscle group effectively (covered in Chapter 3) to sing high notes. You also need to remember it's important to develop both head and chest voice and their integration, as most singing integrates both muscle groups to some degree; that is, most of singing has some degree of activation of both CT muscle group and TA muscle group.

To sing high notes, you must develop a light voice first, not a **belting** voice. Most of the beginners we see in the studio strain and push to reach high notes because they're singing in mixed voice, where both sets of muscles are activated. Some people try to belt those notes, which involves heavy muscular activation and can be damaging to untrained voices. Here are two methods we have found that are effective in training to sing high notes:

Method 1: Start on a lower note, in which your chest voice is activated, and use a chromatic track starting at *A#3* or *A#2* to sing up using **lip rolls/trills** until you can't get any more quality notes. Record your high note. Then repeat this using the vowels: *ah* (as in father), *eh* (egg), *ae* (can), *oh* (snow), *oo* (soup), *ou* (put), *aw* (lost), *ih* (city).

Method 2: Compare the information above to a song that you feel you can't sing, for example, the notes are too high. Is the high note in the song higher than you can sing or are you tensed up and burned out by the time the high note comes? Or is this a mental thing going on? Do you just think the note is too high, so you don't try it? Or do you try and belt the high note and burn out in the process? Or is the movement between chest and head voice creating an over con-traction and a belt/burnout? You've got to be willing to take the time to experiment to find out all of the factors that may be obstacles to you singing those high notes and then train specifically to address those obstacles.

Interestingly, sometimes it's the notes that come before that money note that can trip you up and it's not that you can't hit it accurately. An example is the high note in "Don't Stop Believin'," originally recorded by Journey. For those of you familiar with the tune, the word night is difficult for many singers. We've had our students substitute the vowel ah for the vowel that is sung in the original song at *B4*, and most can sing it if they have a little training under their belts. But when they sing the song, they just can't seem to hit that note. Why? They are exhausted by the time they get to it and the movement from chest to head voice (moving from the notes before night up to that *B4*) can create problems for those who haven't trained for such movements.

Getting up to those high notes can be done – you can do it! Try this:

1. Find out the maximum high note you can actually sing for any period of time using thin **head voice** (**falsetto**-like)

2. Find out if there are vowels that limit that high note even further. Experiment with the vowels listed above.

3. Compare the above information to songs you want to sing that you think are too high for you to sing. If it's too high for you to sing, work on expanding your range and **transpose** the song into a more comfortable range.

4. Train until the muscular movement is more natural/easy, and then move up a **half step** up at a time from the original **key** to train at higher notes and stretch your voice if you want to sing it in the original key.

5. Realize that your voice is organic and changes from day to day just like your body. It isn't a badge of honor to sing a song in the original key. Find a key that maximizes how you sound. Most of the time this will be within a half-step to even two to three **steps** of the original. This is often what artists do while touring. If they are tired or overworked, they will sing a song down a step or two when singing live.

WHAT IS THE BEST EXERCISE FOR INCREASING YOUR RANGE?

The best exercise for increasing your range is as follows. Repeat the exercise daily.

1. **Warmup**.

2. Sing to a chromatic scale starting at *C2* (that is for lower voices) or *C3* (for higher voices) and going up as high as you can go. Use **lip rolls/trills** for beginners and anyone regardless of their singing level who feels stress in their voice—do not strain to get too high. See our website for a chromatic track.

3. Use the same test in exercise above, but use a vowel (ah, eh, oo—pick the most comfortable) and sing up to match as many notes as possible. Do not strain—this is an exercise that should not be pushed too far.

CHAPTER 3

DEMYSTIFYING VOCAL REGISTERS

Sarah is a new vocalist. Her goal is to sing in public, but she has never worked up the nerve. She can match pitch after three months of consistent work but struggles with using her **head voice** to hit those higher notes. Sarah says she doesn't like the way it sounds so she consistently **octaves** down into her chest voice. Sometimes this works and other times it doesn't. She's frustrated with the way her voice sounds, particularly in studio recordings. For the most part, Sarah's issue is mostly psychological in nature. She's avoiding the stress of singing notes she thinks are too high, coupled with her concern about how her head voice sounds. To solve this issue, we assigned a two month-long program of singing in **head voice (CT muscle group)**. The tracks consistently and chromatically move through her break as the notes get higher. In addition, she was assigned to sing almost all songs in her thin head voice during this time frame. Yes, she was resistant at first, but now she is so pleased when she hears more resonance when she uses her head voice and what happens when she combines head and **chest voice**. Her newfound capacity to sing more resonantly across her range gives her new confidence to attack her next challenge: using **mixed voice** and **belting**.

If you're like most beginning vocalists, you read about Sarah thinking, *What the heck is head and chest voice? What's a CT muscle group? When is this going to be explained?* No worries! Once you read this chapter, you'll have all the information you need to understand and converse about vocal registers.

WHAT IS A VOCAL REGISTER?

To answer this question, let's start with a metaphor. Think about the voice as a musical instrument. Every musical instrument has a vibrating mechanism that produces sound waves. On a guitar, for example, if you tighten a guitar string, the notes produced by that string vibrate faster and are higher in pitch than before it was tightened. The size of string also matters. If you tried to get the thickest guitar string as tight as the thinnest string so they sounded the same, this would place tremendous strain on the guitar neck and likely bend, break, or damage it, or the string would break.

Warning: Some basic physics coming your way! The more mass you move, the more energy is required. More energy is also needed to move something faster. In our thick guitar string example, making it produce higher notes requires it to vibrate or move faster, which means increased energy and stress on the instrument. The same can be said for our **vocal folds**. (The terms vocal folds and vocal cords are used interchangeably throughout this book.) The tighter you tune a string or stretch a vocal cord, the more stress is placed on the vocal cord. And our vocal folds produce higher pitches when they are stretched. So, if you force high notes by stretching your vocal folds beyond their capacity, you can damage them. That is why it is so important for you to work out your voice on a regular basis so you can increase the strength and flexibility of your vocal folds. If you still don't understand the idea of stress, think about how you can twiddle a pencil back and forth so fast that it becomes a blur. How much muscle would be required to do this with something larger, like a baseball bat? A lot. When you sing higher notes, your vocal folds vibrate faster, and when you belt you force the whole structure to vibrate. Faster vibration means more stress. Think of G forces, like an astronaut being launched into space.

Our voice's vibrating mechanisms are made up of muscular systems. As with the guitar, high pitches (fast vibration) are determined by the tightness of your vocal folds. Our vocal cords are amazing parts of our bodies. They can be stretched, thickened, or thinned, which changes the actual source of the sound waves. The muscular combinations are endless! While this complexity gives singers lots of options for note choices, it can also be complicated to learn how to control those muscles to produce the kind of notes we want.

While some voice coaches use the terms head voice or chest voice loosely, with little definition when discussing vocal registers, here are the scientific definitions. *M0*, *M1*, *M2*, and *M3* are the designations for these registers. We seldom talk about these scientific abbreviations with our students, we want to make sure you're aware of them and have an understanding of their corresponding labels in case you see them in other references. Please note that the following is what is known in vocal science as of this writing. This scientific discipline is continually evolving.

M0: Slowest vibrating; slow and easy vibration; the full vocal fold tissue vibrates. This is also called vocal fry. In our studio, we call it zombie voice. If you are a horror aficionado (one of us is a hardcore horror fan!), think of the sound that the ghost made in the 2004 movie *The Grudge*. Vocal fry is atonal. In other words, you aren't hitting a pitch when you are using vocal fry.

M1: Medium speed; speaking voice and most of our singing range; the full vocal fold tissue vibrates. This is often referred to as chest voice and a good portion of head voice. Hang in there! We will get to chest and head voice in a bit.

M2: Fast speed; high notes (including, but not limited to, falsetto); only the outer covering or inner edges of the vocal fold tend to vibrate. There's not a lot of tissue involved in this vibration, but it is vibrating fast. Think of Prince singing *Kiss* or Frankie Valli singing *December 1963 (Oh What a Night)*.

M3: Whistle register; very high notes; inner edges of the vocal folds tend to vibrate. Think Mariah Carey. These are generally above *D6*, but there can be some overlap with falsetto.

Now that you understand what vocal registers are, let's define each one separately.

WHAT IS HEAD VOICE?

A quick definition of head voice is the high notes you can sing above your speaking voice and above your **vocal break** to the point to where you must use **falsetto** to reach the notes. Singing in your head voice is a moving target, depending on your development as a vocalist and how much you force the notes through belting.

Graphic 3.1 shows the average range on piano for chest voice, head voice, falsetto, and whistle register. The ranges below are approximate based on averages and may or may not accurate for you.

Graphic 3.1

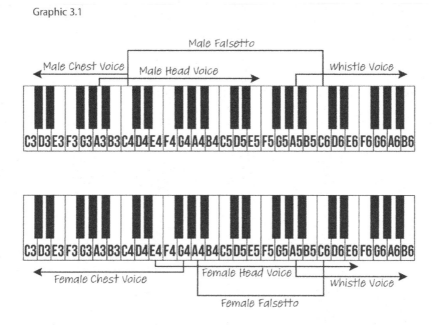

Here is another way to think about the various vocal registers and their corresponding notes based on biological sex:

Chest Voice: That is speaking voice below *C4* for males and below *G4* for females.

Head Voice: That is *A3* to *E5* for males and about *E4* to *C6* for females.

Falsetto: *C4* to *C6* for males. Some researchers say there is no female falsetto, but we don't subscribe to that. Falsetto for women is breathy and light, usually above *A4* to *C5*.

Whistle Register: *A5* and up for both males and females.

Head voice is controlled by the CT muscle group (crichothyroid muscle group). When singing in head voice, the vocal folds are thinned out and the outer covering and inner edges vibrate. Head voice also includes mixed voice and belting, and this can be confusing to some singers. So why do we include mixed voice and belting under the head voice designation? This is due to the absolute frequency associated with the notes. Mixed voice and belting require head voice frequency and chest voice musculature. Refer to Chapter 1 for our discussion on notes and their frequencies.

One of our students used to refer to her head voice as her fake voice because it sounded thin and lacked richness, so she would consistently push her chest voice to hit higher notes, which caused fatigue. We worked to get her to use the light, thin head voice to reach higher notes and to train specifically on using head voice. After a few months of training, she didn't call her head voice fake anymore! It sounded much more resonant after her diligent work.

WHAT IS CHEST VOICE?

Chest voice is a bit easier to understand and find than head voice. Chest voice is your speaking voice. Speak in a normal voice and say something— say *ah* in a natural, non-pushed tone. Just like you realized something . . . an epiphany, *Ah!* Then sing that *ah* comfortably, right in your vocal sweet spot. That is your chest voice. Your chest voice also has a range associated with it, and it's important to find yours. Lucky for you, we've included a way for you to find your chest voice range at the end of this chapter.

WHAT IS MIXED VOICE?

Mixed voice is the use of chest voice musculature above your vocal break. Your vocal break is the point where you are forced to transfer control from the TA (thyroarytenoid) muscle group that controls chest voice to the CT (crichothyroid) musculature that controls head voice. So mixed voice involves using chest voice to hit higher notes so you can sound more powerful and resonant. Unless you regularly train your voice, singing in mixed voice above your break can be taxing, and some people strain and cough which isn't conducive to a good performance.

A popular perspective is that most singing voice is mixed voice. We've found contradictory information on this issue, and most discussions about mixed voice on the Internet are referring to the resonance that you get from engaging chest voice musculature when singing higher notes.

Remember our student who called her head voice her fake voice because it wasn't as resonant as her chest voice? She was consistently using mixed voice to hit higher notes, and she would poop out and start coughing in the middle of a song! For her, the higher the note, the more coughing she did. Many beginning vocalists experience the same thing, so get to work on that head voice! Having a strong head voice can make such a difference in how you sound, and it opens up the variety of songs you can competently sing.

WHAT IS THE VOCAL/VOICE BREAK?

Your break refers to the point where chest voice ends (i.e., you are only using your TA musculature, see the above discussion) and head voice/mixed voice starts to engage. This is also called *passaggio* (sounds so fancy!). For most males, this is *A♯3* to *E4*, and for most females, this is from *F4* to *C5*. Realize that most people reading this will be in that range; however, there are exceptions, and until you have worked out your voice for at least a year, your break may be difficult for you to find by yourself.

WHAT IS THE BEST WAY TO FIND MY PASSAGGIO AND HEAD VOICE?

To find your passaggio and head voice, use a pitch detector as explained below. But don't worry about finding your break until you can reliably match pitch.

Once you can consistently match pitch, it's likely that you will begin to naturally hear and feel your break. Typically, your break will be in the upper half or last third of your range, where it is difficult to hit notes with without a voice flip or crack. Once you are through your break, which will likely be a range of a few notes, you can transition into head voice. When you are in head voice, all of a sudden singing those higher notes becomes easier until you get to the top of your range. Then it gets more difficult again.

Here's a sure-fire way to find your passaggio and head voice! Use a **chromatic** scale or a keyboard and sing each note. (See our website for a chromatic track you can use.) Start as low as you can go, taking your time. You don't have to rush. Then, continue to play/listen to the notes and match the pitch, checking your accuracy on a pitch detector. (Don't forget to **warmup** first!) As you go up the scale chromatically, males (this is typical, but you could be different) should start having difficulty singing the notes between *B3* and *E4*. You will strain to get above this point. At this point, release into a light singing voice or as our student called it, your fake voice. Remember, your head voice is thinner than your chest voice. You can use a hum or **lip roll** if you find yourself straining. For females (again, this is a generality), you will start to feel that same weight or strain at about *F4* to *B4*. When you feel the weight, switch over to light singing in your head voice. For all singers, remember that the goal is to find your break and head voice and not sound like a singing star. So if you get a voice flip, crackle, or strange sound, don't worry. In fact, you should rejoice—ta dah!—you've found your vocal break (or for you fancy people, your passaggio).

This is a fantastic exercise because it is integrated. While voice training is super important, no one wants to spend all day doing it, so finding exercises that get at two or more skills simultaneously can save time. (Crystal calls this double dipping!) This exercise helps you increase pitch-matching skills because you're singing to a track or keyboard while having visual feedback to check your accuracy. While you're doing that, you're paying close attention to how you sound and how your body feels (particularly your voice muscles) as you sing the notes. This is a great exercise to do daily until you can accurately match pitch and work smoothly through your break.

See Graphic 3.2 for the authors' chest voice, mixed voice range, passaggio, head voice, and other information that may be helpful in you charting your own break.

Graphic 3.2

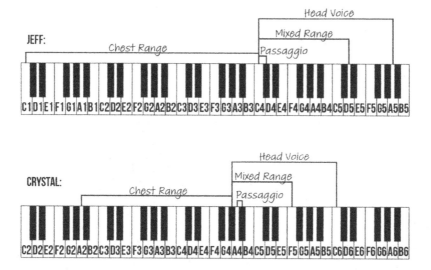

CHAPTER 4

BREATHING AND SINGING: POWERING YOUR VOCAL INSTRUMENT

When Naveah came to our studio for her vocal assessment, her ability to match was above average, making her pitch-matching skills ahead of her vocal development and training level. In her first few months of training, she matched pitch at what would be expected for a someone in their second year in our program. But Naveah's breath control was a different story. She learned to rely on breathiness to help her match pitch and, unfortunately, this became a crutch. For Naveah, this was not a strategic breathy effect but a waste of breath.

This breath wasting happens not at the diaphragm (what many coaches would claim) but at the vocal folds. You must control the stream of air escaping from the lungs, because this powers your voice. Naveah was consistently breathing in the middle of longer phrases, as she didn't have enough breath to carry her through; however, rather than telling her to breathe deeper and lower (what her previous coach told her—and it didn't work), we had her sing louder. This increase in volume required a more vigorous closing of her vocal folds, which allowed less air to escape. This increased the amount of time she could sing and avoided those mid-phrase breath breaks. Naveah thought that it was magic, but we explained that she just needed to avoid excess breath leaking out. Your breath is what powers your song, and learning how to meter and control it is vital.

WHAT IS BREATH SUPPORT IN SINGING?

Breath support is one of the most critical yet misunderstood singing skills. Many of the online gurus talk about more breath support without explaining what it means. Breath support from an operational perspective consists of four separate factors:

1. breathing in;

2. engaging core musculature;

3. controlled phonation (i.e., singing or making sound);

4. recovery/repeat.

Most online resources talk about breathing with the diaphragm, but all breathing, even incorrect breathing, involves the diaphragm. What the singer wants to avoid is using the upper chest area to breathe. If your shoulders are moving up or tensing when you breathe, you need to engage your abdominal muscles, intercostal muscles, and back muscles. Chest breathing tenses the vocal apparatus and makes your singing sound tight, which is the opposite of what you want to do! Ideally, your neck and shoulders should be relaxed when singing. This even goes for emo or heavy metal screaming! Relax . . . Otherwise you will over tense, over compress, and run out of gas early. Your posture is super important in this relaxation. Check out the picture below demonstrating both poor and proper posture.

Graphic 4.1

Poor Posture   Proper Posture

The next picture shows you how to locate those abdominal, intercostal, and back muscles. Place your thumbs right below your ribs in back and your index fingers just below the ribs in front. Now lay your other fingers below your index finger on your abdomen. Breathe in, inflating your lower lungs so you can feel the pressure of your abdomen expanding against your hands. Breathe in and out like this for a couple of minutes, getting used to the sensation. The idea is to have a solid core.

On the in breath, your gut isn't concave – it should be pooched out (that's Crystal's terminology). You are filling up the lungs entirely, from the top to the bottom. If your shoulders and chest are moving, you aren't inflating the entirety of the lungs. Until breathing this way becomes second nature, make this exercise a regular part of your singing workout routine. Here is a picture of Jeff showing how to find your intercostal musculature from front and back.

Graphic 4.2

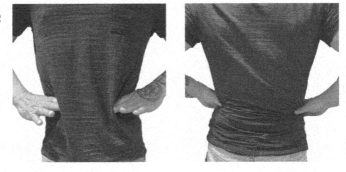

WHAT IS BREATH CONTROL IN SINGING?

Breath control is the metering of your breath using your vocal folds, and is different than breath support. Think of blowing up a balloon—that is breath support. Now think of gradually letting out the air in a balloon. What is the best way to deflate the balloon slowly? It is by making a very small opening at the end of the balloon. That will make a high-pitched noise while the balloon deflates. If you make a large opening there is little or no pitch, and it deflates quickly. This is the reason that most singers shouldn't try to be breathy. The automatic impulse is to be breathy as a beginning singer to mask the inability to match pitch.

The real problem is that breathiness will not allow you to hold notes or sing lengthier phrases without taking a breath, which can interrupt the flow of the music. Sounding breathy and singing breathy are two different configurations. Experienced singers who sound breathy are much less breathy that you think. In fact, sounding breathy without running out of air requires strong vocal musculature. That is the magic of good technique.

At the end of the chapter is an exercise that will help you with both your breath support and your breath control. Our best advice is to practice not being breathy, even if that is an effect you want to use in your singing. Until you can control your singing, really control your singing by controlling the tension on your vocal folds, you will not master the breath-metering process.

WHY DO I RUN OUT OF BREATH OR GET BREATHLESS WHEN SINGING?

You run out of breath simply because you don't have the appropriate musculature, support, and control of your breathing process. It comes down to your breath support (breathing with relaxed neck and shoulders and a tight core that expands and contracts as you breathe) and the metering of your breath (how much breath is expelled through your vocal folds). You also run out of breath by being breathy. You don't run out of breath by sounding breathy. See the section above for a full explanation.

HOW SHOULD I BREATHE WHEN I SING?

You should breathe deliberately, use your lower abdominal, intercostal, and back muscles while relaxing your neck and shoulders. As a beginning singer, make breathing exercises part of your workout routine. And understand that this takes some time. As with all skills involved in singing, patience is key, as improvements may be incremental. Once you're able to consciously control your breathing, the process slowly becomes automatic; in other words, it becomes something you do unconsciously. Once that occurs, you will be able to focus on other factors.

As a beginner or even intermediate singer, you've got to pay attention to a whole bunch of stuff (breath control, pitch matching, lyrics, timing, vowels usage . . . the list goes on and on!) to improve your singing performance. And that can be overwhelming. The consensus of the scientific evidence says that when multitasking—forcing our brain to constantly switch gears to bounce back and forth between tasks that are complex and require undevoted attention—we become less efficient and more likely to mess up. The advice from experts is that you should tackle one thing at a time, and we couldn't agree more.

So, what does that mean for singing? Say you are singing a new song as a beginning vocalist. During the first run-through, focus your attention on matching pitch. During another take, focus on your breathing. The third time you sing it, pay close attention to your dynamics. Singing is a complex set of skills and cognitive processes, so you can't just breathe during a song, you've got to match pitch, remember the lyrics, stay in time, and so on. But you can choose to pay closer attention to only one skill until it is automatic.

HOW DO I GET MORE BREATH WHILE SINGING?

You've got to train for this specifically! You get more breath by focusing on it as part of your practice routine.

This is one of the secrets of singing well. Good vocalists do not allow technique to be a chance acquisition. Great vocalists train to be proficient in the techniques needed to support their singing goals. This simplifies the training process.

So, what do you need to practice most? Your practice priority should be what you need most to improve your singing this week, and you should know that will change over time. Get a prioritized list and then practice that first. Focus on that intensely. Once you have that technique until control, then it will be self-evident when the next item on the list comes up. So, if breath support and control are holding you back, make that a priority in your singing workout routine. Systematically focus your efforts there. Once you are proficient in that area, you may begin to notice that your pitch tends to be sharp when singing, so shift your focus to pitch correction and move breath support down the list.

WHAT IS SINGING FROM YOUR DIAPHRAGM VERSUS FROM YOUR CHEST?

Although many Internet voice coaches talk about diaphragmatic breathing with few details, it is breathing low (i.e., not shallow chest breathing) and singing with proper core support (see Graphics 4.1 and 4.2). In other words, you want musculature engagement below the rib cage and relaxation above it. Your throat should be relaxed, just using the muscles needed to engage the right pitch. If your neck is flexed, you're not getting the most out of your singing. Flexing your neck and tensing your shoulders (this often happens unconsciously) can exhaust you, wear out your voice, lead to straining, and, in the worst case, damage your vocal equipment. Like an Olympic skater, a good vocalist trains to do things other people can't do while making those things look easy and effortless.

You've got to pay attention to your body to assess if you are tensing your shoulders and neck. Many singers focus on other things like, *What will people think about my singing? I hope I don't screw this up! I still don't sound like I want to after two weeks of working out!* Your body is your instrument and, just like you would pay attention to your guitar's condition and tuning, focusing on how your body feels while singing is vitally important. This is easier said than done. Some tricks to consider are putting up a note or some other sign that you can see when you are working out that says something like, "Pay attention to my shoulder tension!" (And make sure you change the color or position of the note or you will habituate to it, and it will become invisible.) Wow! Who knew something so seemingly automatic—breathing—would require so much work?

WHAT ARE THE BEST EXERCISES FOR BREATHING WHEN SINGING?

The best exercises for learning breath control while singing challenge the various metrics of breathing. What are these metrics?

1. Total breath capacity: This is based on lung size, but it can be increased by strengthening the peripheral core muscles.

2. Core muscle negative rep training: This is the capability to hold a stable core, not letting your core collapse, while you are pushing up on your diaphragm which gives a very even, very predictable air flow to the vocal folds.

3. Vocal fold metering: You practice this with varying dynamics so you know when you are bleeding too much air. Sounding breathy and being breathy are two different states. You must be able to use a breathy sound while maintaining an airflow that will carry you through phrases comfortably.

4. Phrase estimation training: You need to know how phrases are going to play out from a performance perspective. Will you be

able to maintain airflow through the phrase without stopping and gulping air? This is critical for smooth singing.

The best exercise for a beginner is to make a continuous sound and measure the length of time you can continue to make a sound. Use your phone or other timer to keep track. Take a deep breath, sing a note using a vowel like *ah,* and start the timer. Do this daily for two weeks. After that, add it to your practice routine when there is a need to improve this skill. Remember, you've got to change up your practice routine every few weeks for the best results. At the beginning, it may only be ten seconds, but you should quickly increase your capacity, all while holding a solid core. More advanced exercises measure your capacity at various notes in your range to find problem areas.

CHAPTER 5

SINGING INTERVALS: MOVING BETWEEN NOTES IN SONGS

Steven had taken singing lessons on and off for a couple of years. His primary instrument was guitar, but he wanted to sing and play at the same time. When he came to the studio, he shared that the quality of his singing would slip when he was concentrating on playing the guitar. Although he could match pitch well using a **chromatic** scale, singing intervals required in the songs he was working on was a considerable challenge.

We helped Steven solve his issues by specifically training on interval movement for a six-month period, which greatly improved his capacity to sing common melody lines. He also trained on basic melody lines (basically a series of intervals) that moved from low to high chromatically, which forced him to learn where his **break** was so he could move easily from **chest** to **head** voice. Once the specific exercises were put in place, his improvement was consistent from week to week.

As with most students we see, the weekly improvement waned the longer he worked on the same exercise, and we've found that about two weeks for each exercise group had the maximum amount of return. Steven prioritized intervals in his workouts, and like most students, he needed one to two weeks training on a particular interval exercise group before it was time to mix it up. (This assumes voice training at least five days per week.) Too short of a period doesn't maximize the learning from specific exercises, and too long spent on a particular exercise can result in very slow improvement, if any at all.

Another consideration is that doing the same exercises, even targeted exercises, for longer than a month can result in slow progress. Doing the wrong exercises can, at worst, put your vocal health at risk and, at best, waste your time and frustrate you. Voice building is like bodybuilding, in that you've got to have the right exercises at the right time or your voice will not end up being what it could be.

As a side note, you can overtrain your vocal muscles just like you can any other muscle group. About 90 percent of our students tend to flourish with this two-week period for new exercises. Keep in mind that exercises are additive. For example, if a student needs two weeks to work on a basic interval (minor second, for example), then the next exercise should build on that. The student could add another interval (major second, for example) or utilize that interval in a melody line. There are many combinations of training, but learning what is best for you is important. We cautioned Steven that switching exercises too often can also retard one's vocal development, so each student must find their own sweet spot. That is why we suggest seeking the advice from a reputable, experienced voice coach at various points along your singing journey. More to come on that topic in Chapter 12. Let's dig in on this concept of intervals!

WHAT ARE INTERVALS IN MUSIC?

Intervals are a simple concept. An interval is merely the distance between two notes. This is easy to see on a keyboard. For example, on a piano, the notes that are right next to each other are a minor second apart. So, if you are starting from the note *A,* a minor second would be the note *A♯* which is the note right next to *A.* If there is one piano key (i.e., note) in between *A* and another note as you go up the keyboard, it is a major second, which in this example would be *B*. If there are two keys between the target note and another note as you go up the keyboard, it is a minor third.

The intervals that are important for the average singer are listed below in order. Their names as well as the abbreviations are given. Note that in the abbreviations, lower case m stands for minor and upper-case M stands for major.

1. minor second (m2)

2. major second (M2)

3. minor third (m3)

4. major third (M3)

5. perfect fourth (P4)

6. tritone (TT)

7. perfect fifth (P5)

8. minor sixth (m6)

9. major sixth (M6)

10. minor seventh (m7)

11. major seventh (M7)

12. **octave** (8va, which is the octave above. Refer to Chapter 1 for a discussion of octaves.)

Remember, these intervals are the distances from a particular reference note. Graphic 5.1 shows the distances from *C* on the keyboard. While the reference note may change, the distances between each interval and that new reference note are the same.

Graphic 5.1

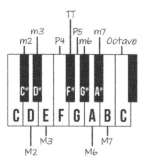

One of the simplest ways to learn intervals is to associate them with the melodic movement of various songs. To help you hear these intervals in popular music, check out the tables below.

Table 5.2 Examples of Songs with Each Major Interval

Interval	Song Example & Notes that Make Up the Major Interval (ascending from low to high)
Major second	Second and third notes in *Happy Birthday*
Major third	First two notes in *When the Saints Go Marching In*
Perfect fourth	First two notes in *Amazing Grace*
Perfect fifth	Second and third notes in *Twinkle Twinkle Little Star*
Major sixth	First two notes in *For He's a Jolly Good Fellow*
Major seventh	First two notes in *Take on Me* by A-Ha
Octave	First two notes in *Somewhere Over the Rainbow*

Table 5.2: Examples of Songs with Each Minor Interval

Interval	Song Example & Notes that Make Up the Minor Interval (ascending from low to high)
Minor second	First two notes in the theme from the movie Jaws
Minor third	First two notes in the guitar riff from *Smoke on the Water* by Deep Purple
Minor sixth	Third and fourth notes in *The Entertainer*
Minor seventh	Second and third notes in the chorus of the *Winner Takes It All* by ABBA

You may wonder why there is no entry for tritone in the tables. The tritone interval is one that's uncommon due to its dissonant sound. Historically known as the devil's interval or *diabolus musica*, it has a foreboding and creepy vibe. Interestingly, the first two notes of *The Simpsons* theme song make up a tritone!

WHY ARE INTERVALS IMPORTANT?

Intervals are an extremely important, yet neglected, part of singing training. Most people hear interval training and they say, *I don't want to do that, I just want to sing*! Singing is intervals. All melodies in a song are a series of intervals. In other words, the notes in the melody move from a reference note to another note. Once you master the basic intervals, then singing songs becomes easier, as you are capable and confident that you can make the musical movement in any melody line.

If you have trouble with a specific interval, practice that interval. We've said it before, and we'll say it again: Train on what is most difficult for you! Don't waste your valuable workout time singing things you have already mastered. We understand that it can be frustrating to work on things you aren't good at singing. It feels much better to sing what we know. But work through that discomfort and you will reap rewards!

WHAT IS THE BEST WAY TO LEARN AND PRACTICE INTERVALS?

We have found the following steps to be an effective way to learn intervals.

1. First, learn to match pitch well. You can't accurately sing an interval that is comprised of two notes unless you can sing one note on pitch. We can't emphasize this step enough.

2. Sing the intervals from the same root or reference note. For example, if you are just starting to work with intervals, make sure that reference note is easy for you. Middle C is a good place to start. Middle C is in the fourth octave and is also referred to as C4. You can use a keyboard for this and sing the vowel 'ah.' Play middle C, match the pitch, and then play the minor second, which is the next key and match that pitch. Then move onto the major second which is the key after the minor second. Play middle C and then play the major second, matching those pitches. Move on up the keyboard chromatically until you get to the octave.

3. You can also go to our website and access the practice tracks that are available if you don't have a keyboard or if you want to practice without a keyboard.

4. And keep up the good work! You may find that you must train on one interval at a time until you master it and move on to the next interval. Don't rush it. Remember, with musical studies there is no final destination because you can keep getting better and better. Learning to sing is all about focusing on the journey.

CHAPTER 6

SINGING HARMONIES: COMBINING TWO OR MORE NOTES TO MAKE SWEET MUSIC

Elizabeth is a thirty-something mother of two who has decided to finally pursue her passion for singing. Her biggest challenges are time and psychological obstacles that include a harsh inner critic (sound familiar?). She has a beautiful voice but doesn't like the way it sounds. From our experience, Elizabeth isn't alone in this. When she first came to the studio, her singing was often flat, sometimes by as many as three or four steps (i.e., notes) when she sang songs. We knew that Elizabeth had a lot on her plate, so we wanted to come up with a solution that addressed more than one issue so she could progress given the limited amount of time she had to devote to her singing practice.

One of the main issues that needed correction was her pitch matching, and to make the most out of her workout routine, we focused on pitch matching through the lens of harmony. Simply put, harmony is combining two or more notes that are pleasing to the ear. Elizabeth worked on a simple exercise where a single note is played and then she repeated the note. Next, a second note is played that harmonizes with the first note. While that note plays, Elizabeth repeated the first note while the harmony note rang out. Finally, both the root and harmony notes are played together, and the singer repeats the root note.

This was very challenging for Elizabeth at first, because she found it easy to get drawn off the root note (the first note that was played) when she sang the harmony note, but with a few days' practice, she was able to maintain pitch matching for all three iterations of the note. This exercise was then changed to make it more challenging—she had to listen to the root note and instead of singing that note, she would sing the harmonic note. Within three months, Elizabeth was no longer singing a melody two or three steps flat, she knew when she was singing the appropriate pitch and when she wasn't.

Too often singing coaches only provide harmony training to sing harmony parts, without realizing all of the peripheral benefits that it brings. Singing harmony helps the vocalist to sing the correct starting and ending notes in a melody because it helps not only with pitch matching but with **intervals** and ear training all at the same time! This type of training also helps to develop the ability to avoid the common pitfall of matching pitch with other instruments or vocalists who are playing or singing the wrong note, which is very common.

Harmony training is beneficial to all vocalists, as all sing harmony in one way or another. It's just that lead vocalists sing harmony with instruments. In other words, the instruments are often playing chords (two or more notes that sound pleasing together), and the lead vocalist is singing a melody over those chords. The reason that the melody is pleasing to the ear is because it's in harmony with the other instruments. Let's dive into our questions and answers.

WHAT DOES HARMONY MEAN IN MUSIC?

To understand harmony, we need to cover a little music theory. At the beginning of her formal training as a vocalist and guitarist, any mention of music theory made one of the authors—Crystal—want to run and hide! Please know we are going to do everything we can to make this both understandable and applicable, so the words music theory don't sound so daunting and painful! Let's take care of a few definitions.

Scale: A scale is a collection of notes that go together. A scale has intervals (covered in Chapter 5) that create a specific pattern of notes.

Diatonic Scale: Diatonic basically means containing seven, so the diatonic scale has seven notes. The diatonic scale can begin on any note, but the intervals between the notes are the same regardless of what note you start on. Below is the pattern of notes for the major diatonic scale. W signifies whole step and H signifies half step. On a piano keyboard, a whole step has one note in between the first note and the next note. And that note can be either a white or a black key. A half step is the note right next to the previous note.

W W H W W W H

For example, if your starting note is *A*, the next note in the diatonic scale is two notes away—or there is one note between *A* and the next note in the scale which is a whole step. So, the second note in the *A* major scale is *B*. The note that is in between *A* and *B* is *A*♯ (*A*♯ is one of the black keys on the keyboard. Remember, the black keys on the keyboard are sharps and flats.). After *B* (the second note in the scale of *A* major), the next note in the scale would be a whole step away, which would be *C*♯. Notice on the keyboard that *B* and *C* are right next to each other. There is no black key that separates them.

Following the pattern above, the next note in the scale after *C♯* is a half-step away, so it is the note right next to *C♯*, which is *D*. After *D*, we need to go a whole step up and that gets us to *E*. After *E*, we've got another whole step, which lands us on *F♯* (like *B* and *C*, *E* and *F* are right next to each other with no sharps/flats between). After *F♯*, here we go again with another whole step and that gets us to *G♯*. Then, it starts all over again when we go a half step from *G#* to *A*. Whew! We know that for beginners, that's a lot to follow, and we also know you can get this! If Crystal can get it, you can!

One of the ways that she got it was to write the pattern out on a piece of paper (W W H W W W H) and then write a beginning note (such as *A* in the previous example) and work out the sequence of notes.

Graphic 6.1 shows the *A* major scale on a keyboard.

Graphic 6.1

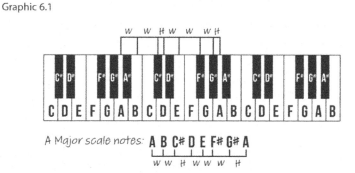

For now, we want you to understand the diatonic major scale, and once you get that, the other scales that are common for vocalists (blues scale, pentatonic scale, and diatonic minor scale) will make more sense with the diatonic major as a reference point.

Okay, now let's get down to the actual question: What does harmony mean in music? Harmony can mean many things, but at its most basic, it means notes that go together within a scale that make pleasing music.

Using the diatonic scale as an example, we can start with one note and choose every other note in the scale until we have three or four notes. This is basic harmony. For example, in the diatonic *A* major scale, the notes are *A, B, C♯, D, E, F♯, G♯*. If we choose *A*, we then skip a note, which gets us to *C♯*, skip another note, and then we are at *E*. That, good people, is an *A* major chord. So if you play *A, C♯,* and *E* together, you've got a chord which is harmony. And regardless of the starting note, say for example *G,* if you choose every other note in the scale starting with *G,* you've got a *G* major chord (and those notes happen to be *G, B,* and *D*). For purposes of this book, harmony is defined as two to four different notes that go together that are pulled from a scale. That's all you need to know right now!

WHAT DOES HARMONY MEAN IN SINGING?

Harmony in singing is very similar to harmony in general. If you've been able to understand the content of this chapter so far, you've got more information than you need to start harmonizing in your vocal pursuits. From choirs singing rock 'n roll to gospel to pop, general vocal harmonies include two to four different notes (or parts). Anything beyond four-part harmony is unusual given their complexity.

Learning to sing harmony isn't easy. Why? Because we have a natural tendency to get pulled off the note we are singing if someone else is singing a different note. It's been theorized that we do this because we are hardwired to fit into the group, and if we're singing a different note, we are outside of the group norm. While harmony is difficult, it certainly is doable with patience and practice.

In our studio, we start our vocalists off singing harmonies in a simple yet effective way. We've used the old song "Lollipop" by the Chordettes to introduce singers to harmonizing. We sing the song in the key of G. The lead singer sings the melody line of the song while the student who is harmonizing holds the note of G. Given the key of the song is G, the G note is a safe one for harmonizing throughout most of the song. Once students can master this, we then move on to more complex harmonies. We found this to be a relatively simple and straightforward way to try out harmonies. And please notice that we said relatively. Singing harmonies requires one to be able to match pitch, have good aural skills, and be patient with the process.

Remember our discussion of chords earlier in this chapter? We used the example of the key of *A* (in other words, the *A* major scale). Chords are created by choosing every other note in the scale. So, if we start on *A* and skip the second note in the scale (which is *B*), the following note is *C#* (the third note in the scale; the second note was skipped). The next chordal note would be *E*, which if the fifth note in the scale. (We skipped the fourth note.) So, a common harmony in the key of *A* would be *A* harmonized with *C#*, or *A* harmonized with *E*.

Graphic 6.2

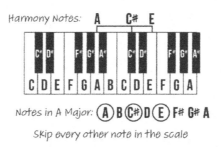

More exotic harmonies can be sung if the harmony singer skips the common notes (*C#* or *E,* if we utilize the example for *A* major). In these harmonies, the root note (*A* in this example) is played/sung, and you don't sing the more common notes. Instead, sing the *G#* either an octave up or an octave down. This is important. If you are singing harmonies, you can sing in the same **octave** as the lead singer, but it can sound better an octave up or an octave down.

WHAT IS THE DIFFERENCE BETWEEN SINGING HARMONY AND MELODY?

Singing melody usually (99 percent of the time) implies that you're a lead singer. You're singing the part that most people sing along with. In the middle ages, everyone who sang harmony sang the melody. This was before the invention of chords where there were coordinated polyphonic melody lines. In English, that means two or more singers sang independent melody lines that harmonized together.

Singing harmony can be as simple as in the "Lollipop" example above or by singing the middle note of the chord or the third note in the chord, possibly an octave apart. For you harmonizers out there, remember this tip! If something doesn't sound right, try it at an octave if you know you are singing the right note, but be sure you are correctly matching pitch first. To sing harmony, you've got to be able to hear a key, hear a note, and know the interval between the notes. For example, if you are singing in the **key** of C (which is made up of the notes C, D, E, F, G, A, B – isn't that cool, no sharps or flats!) and your fellow singer sings a C, and you want to sing a harmony of a C major chord, you would sing and E, G, or B at an octave.

HOW DO VOCAL HARMONIES WORK?

Vocal harmonies work because they are based on the key and the scale that are utilized by the chords in the song. To really understand and be able to sing harmonies, you've got to know your intervals, which were covered in Chapter 5. Remember, an interval is a distance between two notes. Remember that the diatonic scale has seven notes. Let's use C major scale for this example: C major is made up of C, D, E, F, G, A, B (no sharps or flats).

Remember, there are seven notes in the scale. Our lead vocalist will be singing the C note. Our harmony singer will sing either E or a G (as a reminder, you are choosing every other note in the scale so it is C then skip D and go to E and then you are at G (this is the next note after you skip F). But this will also depend on the music in the background. It's assumed for this example that the lead singer is singing over a C, F, or G chord (which are chords in the key), so you can get away with singing any of the notes in the chord that the lead singer is not singing. So rather than focusing on the lead singer, check this out: Sing a note from the music in the background (we're assuming you're not singing a cappella) rather than straight harmonizing with the singer.

Why do this? Because if the singer is singing a note and you harmonize with that note, it could create a tritone (hitting the note in the scale that sounds dissonant) against the chords in the background. And if that happens, it won't sound very good. Easy harmony will focus on the background music. Once you are able to do basic harmonizing and have developed your ear some, you can sing a note in the chord that exists in the background (even an implied chord), rather than harmonizing with the singer directly.

For those of you who ask, yes this can be done by ear as well. Here's the trick: If you want to sing a harmony that works, pick one of the chord tones (notes in the chord) from the background music. This will automatically be in harmony, unless the singer is singing something that is dissonant (doesn't sound like it goes with the music) on purpose. This will work 99 percent of the time!

HOW DO I SING HARMONY WITH SOMEONE?

First, make sure you're able to match pitch well, and you have a good understanding of and can sing your intervals. Know that singing harmonies with someone can be tricky, but with work, you can do it! Some people spend years trying to find the best way to sing harmonies. It can be done by ear, but then if someone asks for a specific type of harmony, you won't know what they're talking about. The best method is to develop a musical understanding (just the basics will do) of what harmony is and then develop your ear to be able to sing harmony.

If you can sing the all of your intervals and are able to sing them when you hear a root note only, you can easily do harmonies. The three necessary steps are:

1. Be able to sing the intervals. (Covered in Chapter 5.)

2. Practice singing one note while someone is singing another note—the root note is a good note to sing against.

3. Practice the intervals above against a real song. Sing along with the root of the chord being played. This is easy, as it is what our ears do by default. Sing one of the intervals above, focusing on minor third, major third, and perfect fourth, perfect fifth. If the note you sing doesn't sound right, then go up by a minor second. If that doesn't sound right, go to the original harmony you were singing and go up by a major second. This should work for you 99 percent of the time.

As a reminder, check out our companion website: YourSingingQuestionsAnswered.com, for a harmony exercise.

CHAPTER 7

RHYTHM AND TIMING: TIMING IS MUSIC

ill has been coming to our studio for weekly lessons for a couple of years and has made monumental gains in his ability to match pitch. He's increased his confidence when singing in front of others as well as being professionally recorded. (That is something we do twice a year for all of our in-person singing students as part of their development.) Bill is fond of singing crooner-type songs that can have unusual timing. Timing—this is Bill's challenge.

He often rushes through lyrics and reports he just "can't get the beat." Without cues from one of us in the studio, it's difficult for him to know when to come in or when to start singing again after an instrumental break in the middle of a song. Although he is resistant to working on his rhythm (many of us don't like working on things that are super hard for us!), rhythm training became his focus for several weeks.

We first asked him to play a basic drumbeat on YouTube that was about fifty beats per minute (BPM). In one-minute increments, he first clapped on the beat. The next minute we asked him to tap his foot to the beat. He continued this until he could do this successfully. Once that was mastered, he clapped on the beat and between the beats (those are eighth notes; we'll explain that later!). We then asked him to do the same thing tapping his foot. Once that was mastered, we moved on to sixteenth notes, which is four claps per beat.

After working with the basic drumbeat with no instrumentation or vocals, his confidence regarding rhythm increased. We then moved on to relatively simple songs where he would clap or tap his foot to the beat while learning to count the beats in the introductory measures so he would know where to come in. After working with this for a few weeks, his sense of timing increased dramatically.

For Bill, this was a long process, but he was patient because he knew it would pay off in the end. It is so important that singers have a sense of embodied rhythm. In other words, they are able to feel the rhythm in their bodies through foot tapping or some other way to keep time using their bodies. You've got to develop your sense of rhythm if you want to be a great singer.

WHAT IS RHYTHM IN MUSIC?

Rhythm is music's pattern over time. All music has rhythm, so it's a necessary component. One can have a musical piece without melody (for example, percussion pieces), but you've got to have rhythm to have a melody. For vocalists, rhythm is as fundamental and important as pitch. The question for the vocalist is what note (pitch) do you sing at what time (rhythm)? The way we look at it, the right note sung at the wrong time is the wrong note!

While we see rhythm and beat are often used interchangeably on the Internet, they are somewhat different. Rhythm consists of patterns of beats that occur repetitively throughout a song. The beat is the most basic part of a song's rhythm, and when you clap your hands or tap your foot, you're identifying the beat or the pulse of the music. Rhythm is the pattern of the notes that flows throughout the song, while the beat is tempo (how fast or slow) that is consistent throughout the piece.

For beginning vocalists, we are most concerned with discerning the beat, which keeps all of the musicians who are playing or singing a particular song in sync with one another. When someone says, "That band sounds tight!" they typically are referring to the fact that the musicians are all in sync with the beat.

WHAT IS SINGING IN TIME, AND WHY IS IT IMPORTANT?

Singing in time is basically singing the right notes at the right time. It is knowing what beat to come in on and how the lyrics correspond with the rhythmic pattern of the song. As we said before, singing out of time is basically singing the wrong notes. When you're a vocalist, there's usually another singer or instrument playing in the background. If you sing a note at the wrong time, you'll change how the melody (what you are singing) sounds over the background track because of the chord (i.e., harmony) changes. The best-case scenario is that you find a new melody that sounds good. On the other hand, the worst-case scenario is that you create a **tritone** that creates enough dissonance that you sound like you don't know what you are doing. Note: a tritone isn't always bad. An intentional tritone that is resolved (quickly goes back to the root note) is good. An unintentional tritone that is unresolved is bad.

Rhythm and timing are as important—or maybe more important—for a vocalist than anyone else in the band, as the vocalist may be leading the action. Lead singers are the ones who often tell the band to slow down or speed up, based on your preferences as the singer. You're out front and know what to do to keep the audience engaged. Vocalists usually drive a song, so it is vital that you're able to keep time. The good news is that of all the musical abilities, developing your rhythm usually takes the least amount of time, but it can be very frustrating, so people tend to ignore it.

As we said before, if you sing the right note at the wrong time, it's the wrong note. Here's an example. Let's start in the key of C major. The notes of the **scale** are C, D, E, F, G, A, B. We've got a simple, two-chord song that uses *C* major and *G* major. The notes associated with each of these chords are (see Chapter 6 on harmony): *C* Major: *C, E, G,* and *G* Major: *G, B, D.*

The vocalist will sing the third of each chord (the middle note), so when the *C* chord is playing they sing *E,* and when the *G* chord is playing they sing *B.* If the singer was just vocalizing and singing ah, it would sound pleasing. But if the singer gets out of time and sings the *E* note when the *G* major chord is played or sings the *B* note when the *C* Major chord is played, it just doesn't sound right. Singing the note of *B* against the *C* chord creates more of a jazzy sound. That's fine if you're singing jazz, but if you are singing rock or pop, it's likely going to sound off. Having a good sense of rhythm and timing can help you avoid these dissonant notes.

CAN ANYONE LEARN RHYTHM?

Anyone can learn to increase their rhythm and timing sense if they invest consistent practice time and can withstand the frustration that comes with it. For Crystal, learning to develop rhythm was the most frustrating part of her musical development. Whenever she attempted to clap out certain beats so she could translate them to the bass, she got all wigged out because she felt so uncoordinated. But she worked through that frustration and stuck with it, and now she's a competent vocalist and bass guitarist!

WHAT IS THE BEST EXERCISE TO IMPROVE MY RHYTHM AS A SINGER?

This journey begins by understanding the pulse or the beat of music. This is as simple as listening to music (or even more basic—working with a metronome) and tapping your foot in time. As we indicated earlier, sense of rhythm is embodied, meaning feeling the rhythm in your body is important. Try this exercise to help you learn, one, how to embody the beat, and, two, learn the names and types of beat subdivision.

YouTube is a great resource for drumbeats and metronomes, so pull up a basic drumbeat at fifty beats per minute (BPM). This drumbeat is likely composed of a kick drum and a snare. The snare drum sounds sharper and more staccato, meaning that duration of the sound is short. The kick drum has a more booming sound. The kick drum will play on beats one and three, which are considered the strong beats, and the snare will play on beats two and four, the weak beats (or backbeat). So, how do we count the beat? Ninety-eight percent of the time, you will be counting in fours: 1, 2, 3, 4, 1, 2, 3, 4 . . . So, listen and tap your foot, clap your hands, or move some other body part (you've got to move something!) in time with each of those four beats. Those four beats are called quarter notes. Count those quarter notes as you listen (again, it's 1, 2, 3, 4).

Once you can do this, you need a couple of tricks. You need to be able to split the beat (quarter note) into equal halves. Those are called eighth notes, which will give you two claps per beat. You can count those notes as "1 and 2 and 3 and 4 and." The ands are between the drumbeats. Then, you need to be able to divide the beat into four equal parts (sixteenth notes). You can count that as "1 ee and uh, 2 ee and uh, 3 ee and uh, 4 ee and uh." Those ee and uhs all happen between those drumbeats. Make sure the time between each clap is equal. For example, many musicians will rush to get two or four claps in, and the last clap rings out longer than the others. If you need to improve your rhythm, this is the exercise for you. Do it for five minutes a day until you've got this mastered. Check out the companion website for some YouTube links to get you started.

CHAPTER 8

SINGING VOWELS: FIX YOUR VOWELS, FIX YOUR SINGING

Nakeem was one of our students who was doing fantastic with his pitch matching. He came to our studio with a burning desire to sing solos in his church but was having difficulty matching pitch. After a few months of work on pitch-matching exercises, he improved greatly and was recorded while singing in church for the first time.

The recording revealed that his timing was good, his pitch matching on point, and his dynamics added to the emotion of the song. Even though he was pleased with these singing metrics, something didn't sound quite right to him, and he couldn't identify it. He brought the recording to the studio, and we were able to diagnose the issue relatively quickly—he needed to understand, study, and work on his singing vowels. This chapter is devoted to the most popular questions people ask about singing vowels.

WHAT IS THE DIFFERENCE BETWEEN SINGING AND TALKING?

Singing and talking are similar in that we use vowels as pitch-dependent sounds and consonants as terminators or shapers of those particular sounds. In other words, consonants interrupt or terminate vowels, and they can also shape the sound of the vowel, depending on which vowel and consonant combination you are using.

The major difference between talking and singing is the use of pitch. For the most part, talking is not pitch dependent, except for evoking emotion (see discussion later). When we talk, we don't think about the pitch we are using, and we tend to use our **chest voice** (TA muscle group) predominately. When speaking, our vowels are short, and talking has a start–stop rhythm (except when you talk to someone who can't stop, so it has a start-keep-going rhythm!). Pronunciation is important when speaking, and one could argue that consonants are more important than vowels when we talk.

On the other hand, singing is pitch dependent. Vowels are held for a longer time, and singing has fewer stops than talking. Singing also involves both the TA (chest voice) and CT (**head voice**) muscle groups, and proper use of vowels is critical, too. Compound vowels are an important aspect of vowel usage in singing. These vowels are also called dipthongs (which sounds more like an insult than a name for vowels) are a combination of two vowel sounds in a single syllable where the sound begins as one vowel and then moves toward another vowel sound. For example, say the word toy. Phonetically, it looks something like this: t-oh-ee. The *oh* and *ee* are the smallest vowel sounds in the combination. These single vowel sounds in a diphthong are called atomic vowels—and no, we don't mean they are radioactive.

Let's contrast speaking and singing the phrase, "and I." It takes approximately one to two seconds to speak these two words, and there is no pitch requirement. Now contrast that with the first two words of the song, *I Will Always Love You* by Whitney Houston. The first pitch Whitney hits is an *E4* (octaves and note names are covered in Chapter 1), and she holds it for approximately one-and-a-half beats. Phonetically, the 'and' looks like this: eh-nd. She then sings the word 'I' by hitting *A* for about four beats, singing the vowel ah, then moving to a *B* then back to *A* while switching her vowel to ee, then to *G♯*, then *A*, then *B* . . . You get the picture! Singing is time and pitch dependent. Speaking is not.

HOW DO YOU PRONOUNCE WORDS WHEN SINGING?

When singing, words are pronounced (generally speaking) with the vowels long, prominent, and with a specific pattern of notes. Consonants are generally abbreviated. Beginning singers often try to speak–sing, and it just doesn't sound right. We encourage our students to rewrite lyrics as a series of specific phonetic sounds. In other words, you're writing out the singing vowels you'll use in the song, along with the consonants. We find this accomplishes two things: First, it can clarify the melody line and timing; and second, it creates the opportunity to substitute vowels that are easier to sing for ones that are harder to sing.

Let's take the first line of the song "Don't Stop Believin'" by Journey: "Just a small town girl." Let's try speaking that line. We have five distinct syllables with a hard stop (consonant of t at the end of just.) Now, let's rewrite this and make it easier to sing by specifying the singing vowels.

"Just a small town girl" becomes: j+y+**ah**+s | T+**ah** | s+m**ah**+l
t+**uh**+**ah**+**uh**+n || g+**uh**+r+l

Try singing this. Focus on the bolded vowels to get the best sound. And the above isn't the only way that this line can be interpreted. The important thing to remember is to sing the best vowel so the melody is stretched and powerful. Much of the time you don't want to sing lyrics as you would speak the words, unless you are singing some sort of story song (think of Johnny Cash's "A Boy Named Sue"), rapping, performing in musical theater, or are going for a specific artistic effect. Helping singers in our studio understand how to sing vowels correctly is one of the biggest game changers we see for improving the singing of someone who can competently match pitch.

WHY ARE VOWELS MORE IMPORTANT THAN CONSONANTS IN SINGING?

Vowels carry (for the most part) the song, or the melody. Consonants generally do not. There are semi-occluded consonants (partially closed mouth) like *M* or *N* that can carry melody, but most of the musical sounds are vowels that are generated with the singer's mouth open. Singers may even choose to drop consonants when they sing. Going back to the example of "Don't Stop Believin'" by Journey, the second line is "Living in a lonely world." It is a good idea when singing that line to drop the *g* at the end of living and the *d* at the end of world. Give it a shot—try singing the line with the consonants and then without them. When you sing that *g*, it basically stops the sound and makes it sound choppy. Which sounds better to you?

WHAT ARE THE SINGING VOWELS?

There are different schools of thought as to what the singing vowels are, but for the most part, the experts are 90 percent in agreement about singing vowels. The disagreements are small, such as the number of singing vowels—should there be eight, nine, eleven, or fifteen different vowels? As the number of singing vowels increases, the differences between and among them can be slight. We've found that it serves most vocalist's purposes to train on and consider eleven vowels.

The chart below gives the vowel in its phonetic form, an example of a familiar English word that has that vowel sound, and if it is considered atomic. (Atomic vowels are ones that are not a combinations of two or more vowels. Remember that combinations of atomic vowels are also called dipthongs.) Here are the eleven vowels we focus most of our time on in our studio.

Table 8.1: Singing Vowels

Vowel	Example
ee	see
ih	city
oh	toe
ae/a	cat
eh	egg
ah	father
aw	saw
uh	run
oo	who
ou	woman
ai	eye-ah and ee

WHAT IS VOWEL MODIFICATION IN SINGING?

Vowel modification is changing the vowel or emphasizing a different vowel than is expected in spoken language. For example, if you were pronouncing the word 'city,' this would be s-ih-t-ee. This is difficult to sing in many circumstances (explanation appears in the next paragraph). One way of making this sound better is this: s-**ih**-d-**eh** or s-**eh**-d-**eh**.

You may be wondering, *Why change the ee to eh?* The ee may sound harsh, depending on the note you are trying to hit, and be difficult to sing in higher octaves. Try it out and see what you think.

Combining articulation and melody can be simplified by merely switching up a single vowel. That's why vocalists often slur their vowels. The primary goal is to sing on pitch to communicate melody and emotion, and not to properly pronounce words (again, there are some exceptions we noted above). Some vowels are easier to sing than others, and this requires some trial and error. The exercise at the end of this chapter can help you as you experiment with various vowels.

HOW DO I SHAPE MY MOUTH WHEN SINGING VOWELS?

There are two primary facial positions singers use. The fancy name voice coaches use for facial position is embouchure. (Pronounced ahm-buh-shoe-er.) The first position is vertical. You drop your jaw without tilting your head back. The dropping of the jaw promotes relaxation, which is necessary for proper enunciation and singing, but you don't want to open too widely or exaggerate this movement. Experiment with this. This position provides a warmer, bigger sound as you're increasing mouth size. Some classical singers even push their lips out to get a bit more space to resonate. Below is a picture of Jeff with vertical embouchure that can be used in contemporary singing.

Graphic 8.2

The second position is horizontal. This position does not require you to drop your jaw, as with the first position. You open your mouth and position your upper lip so that your top teeth are showing. Think of this as showing off your canines! While you might think the position looks a little weird, the resulting sound makes it worth it. Horizontal embouchure is pictured below.

Graphic 8.3

The horizontal position tends to be more energetic and sounds brighter than the first position. Brighter means more high tones and mid-tones come through than lower, warmer tones. This position tends to be used more often than the vertical position in contemporary singing. It is the exact opposite for the classical singer: Classical singers tend to use vertical embouchure more often.

WHAT ARE GLOTTAL STOPS?

Glottal stops are the violent crashing together of the vocal folds. This is usually a result of trying to be very aggressive in your first note execution; however, it can be damaging to your vocal health over time. If you listen closely, you can hear a popping sound as the vocal folds crash together. To avoid this put a short breath of air, think an *h*, in front of a vowel. Instead of singing ah with a hard attack, resulting in a glottal stop, sing h + AH and the raise the volume. This should minimize or eliminate your glottal stops.

WHAT IS THE BEST EXERCISE FOR LEARNING TO PROPERLY SING VOWELS?

Before we give you an exercise, here is the order of tasks when learning to properly use and substitute vowels.

1. Get the vowel right—stay on the proper vowel. The tendency for a beginner is to fall back into uh.

2. Initiate and maintain melody.

3. Initiate proper facial position (experiment with the two embouchures).

4. Substitute for vowel appropriately. Try different vowels to see what sounds the best.

5. Move between vowel and consonant properly. That means sometimes you will drop a consonant. For example, the word land. If you were singing this, you would stay on the *a* (as in cat) longer than the *n*, and drop the *d*.

Here is the exercise: First, familiarize yourself with the singing vowels. Know them by heart. Sing each vowel to a chromatic track (see our website) one after the other until you are familiar with how each vowel sounds with lower and higher pitches. You likely don't want to run through all eleven vowels in one practice session, but do a few at a time. Remember the concept of 'double dipping' we talked about earlier. This is a perfect example! You are working on both your pitch matching and your vowels!

CHAPTER 9

KEYS AND SCALES: BASIC MUSIC THEORY FOR THE BEGINNING VOCALIST

66 "I don't really want to learn any music theory. I just want to sing for fun." We can't tell you how many times we've heard that in our studio. At one point in time, Crystal said the same thing! Why? Because when we hear the words "music theory," some of us get anxious. We're worried we won't understand. We don't want to look stupid. But when Crystal learned that music theory was basically just a description of what sounds good, her attitude changed. If we can learn about the ingredients that make our singing sound awesome, why not learn more about it! So let's dive in. These are the questions most asked about music theory as a beginning vocalist.

WHAT IS A SCALE IN MUSIC?

Simply, a scale is a collection of notes that sound good together. The notes that go together are pleasing to the ear when combined in the right order. A scale has **intervals** that create a specific pattern of notes. Intervals refer to the space between notes. Think about a keyboard. An example of an interval would be one key between notes (and that is just one example).

In Western music, the most referenced scale is the **diatonic scale**, which has seven notes. The major and minor scales are derived from the diatonic scale. Okay, wait a minute . . . isn't this book for beginners? This is supposed to be simple! Let's do some translation from music theory to plain English.

In any scale, the distance between the notes is important. The diatonic scale includes five whole steps and two half steps, and it's the order of these notes and their intervals that are important. Let's look at a piano keyboard. A whole step has one note (or keyboard key) in between the first note and the next note. A half step is the note right next to the previous note. For the guitarists out there, a whole step has a fret in between the two notes and a half step means the frets are right next to each other.

There are many different types of scales derived from the diatonic scale, but we're going to focus on only two: major and minor. If you get a good understanding of these two scales, that will serve you very well as a vocalist—you will know what sounds good when those you're playing with don't know what to sing or why to sing something differently! It's liberating to have a little knowledge! Imagine flying a plane while blindfolded. A person guides you by telling you exactly what to do, but you don't know where you're going or why you need to use the controls they tell you to use. Then imagine having that blindfold removed. Suddenly you can fly on your own, you can choose your destination, and you're free to fly! This is what music theory does. In fact, let's not call it music theory, let's call it the Musical Map to Freedom! The first stop on this map is a review of the major scale.

This scale is the more often than not the reference for talking about other scales. Let's take C for example. C♯ is a **half-step** (H) away from C and D is a **whole step** away from C. The intervals for the major scale are shown below, where W represents whole and H represents half. Although we covered some of this content in a previous chapter, repetition is key in learning music theory.

W W H W W W H

Here is another example using *C* major, with the distances between each of the notes presented in parentheses: *C* (W) *D* (W) *E* (H) *F* (W) *G* (W) *A* (W) *B*. Here it is on a keyboard.

Graphic 9.1

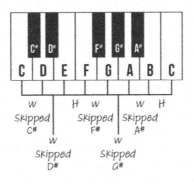

This pattern for the major scale is going to stay the same no matter what note you start on. For example, if your starting note is *A*, the next note in the diatonic scale is two notes away—or there is one note between *A* and the next note in the scale. So, the second note in the *A* major scale is *B*. The note that is in between *A* and *B* is *A♯* which is one of the black keys on the keyboard. (Remember, the black keys on the keyboard are sharps and flats.) After *B* (the second note in the scale of *A* major), the next note in the scale would be a whole step away, which would be *C♯*. Notice on the keyboard that *B* and *C* are right next to each other. There is no black key that separates them. That goes for any *B* or *C* anywhere on the keyboard.

Following the pattern above, the next note in the scale after *C♯* is a half-step away, so it is the note right next to *C♯*, which is *D*. After *D*, we need to go a whole step up and that gets us to *E*. After *E*, we've got another whole step, which lands us on *F♯* (like *B* and *C*, *E* and *F* are right next to each other with no sharps or flats between). After *F♯*, here we go again with another whole step and that gets us to *G♯*. Then, it starts all over again when we go a half step from *G♯* to *A*, which is the **octave**. Whew! We know that for beginners, that's a lot to follow, and we also know you can get this! If Crystal can get it, you can! Graphic 9.2 is a diagram of a keyboard depicting both the *C* and *A* major scales so you can see the actual distances. Remember, the major scale pattern stays the same no matter what note you start on.

Graphic 9.2

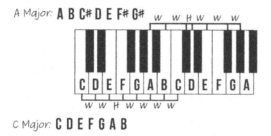

For singers, a common reference for singing the major scale is called solfege or the "Do re mi fa sol la ti do" song. (You're singing that in your head right now, aren't you?) That's the major scale! It sounds bright and happy. If the major scale is cheerful, the minor scale is the major scale's sad and moody counterpart. Just like the major scale, the minor scale has seven notes, but the intervals are different. Here are the intervals for the minor scale:

W H W W H W W

So, let's start on *A* again. A whole step from *A* is *B*, which is the second note. A half step from *B* is *C* (remember, *B* and *C* are right next to each other on the keyboard, so they are just a half step apart). A whole step from *C* is *D*. A whole step from *D* is *E*. A half step from *E* is *F* (just like *B* and *C*, *E* and *F* are only a half step apart. From *F*, a whole step would be *G*. From *G*, a whole step would be *A*, so we end up back at the **octave**. (Octaves are covered in Chapter 1.) Graphic 9.3 shows it on the keyboard.

Graphic 9.3

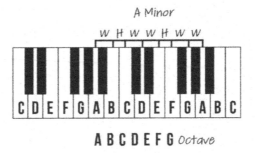

Once you learn the major and minor scale, the other scales really aren't that different musically—the other scales are scales that are more minor or less minor, more major or less major. The pentatonic scale even has fewer notes—it's got five notes. Really, when you learn the major and minor scale, you have learned about 80 percent of everything you need to know about scales. And going into modes is beyond the scope of our discussion—just take our word for it. Learn the distances in the major scale and the minor scale. The goal is to be able to sing the scale if we give you a starting note; for example middle *C*, can you sing the *C* major scale? Can you sing the *C* minor scale?

Again, there are many other scales that singers should know (pentatonic, blues, etc.), but they are beyond the scope of this chapter and book. You'll just have to get another one of our books for that explanation! The two most important scales are the major and minor scales, as the major scale is the reference for most other scales. Work on knowing and understanding the distances between the notes for the major scale, and that will definitely help you as learn other scales. And if it seems like it's taking you a long time to learn it, don't worry. It takes most people repeated exposure and study for it to sink in (or sing in!).

Just remember that a scale is a collection of notes that go together—we need two pieces of information to describe the scale: one, the beginning note, or root of the scale (we used A and C in the examples above); and two, the distances between the notes.

WHY ARE MUSIC SCALES IMPORTANT IN SINGING?

Without a scale, you have talking—literally. When we limit the range of possible notes in the human range to seven, or five, or another series of intervals that carry an emotional quality and pair it with a rhythmic pattern, you've got a song. A song generally communicates some emotional message, and these are drawn using the raw palate of a scale. The scale is the raw colors that you use to paint a picture. But as a series of seven colors does not make a masterpiece—such as in a Picasso—so a scale is nothing more than raw colors. You use the scale to paint a particular emotional picture. The scale is the box that we play in—at least until we change keys— perhaps modulating to change emotion (in other words, we change keys, which is explained below).

For example, the major scale paints more of an upbeat picture whereas the minor scale is moodier, a little darker. The order of notes is important, too. For example, a song can be in a major scale, and you occasionally add some notes from the minor scale to change the emotional nuance of the song. This is the power of music theory.

There is a lot of theory to learn. Music theory, or as we call it, the Map to Musical Freedom, is currently incomplete. People are still coming up with associations and ways to make new scales and apply them in different ways. As such, learning the basics is important. Could you be an Uber driver who was unable to follow street directions or read street signs? Could you be a racecar driver who could steer, but couldn't press the brake pedal? How about a brain surgeon who didn't know how to use a scalpel and had to use a chainsaw? There's probably a movie about that particular one, but the ideas are important.

Learn the tools of your craft. But here is a caveat: Only learn the tools, the musical tools, that you need right now. Otherwise, you can become paralyzed thinking of all the stuff you need to learn. Right now, if you're a beginner, you need to know what a scale is and what the major and minor scale sound like—that's all. A lot of people quit learning theory because there is so much, but you only need to learn what you need to learn right now!

WHAT DOES THE WORD KEY MEAN IN MUSIC?

A key is the main group of notes that form the harmonic and melodic basis for a piece of music. It can be thought of as the notes that are used in a song. The key is described by the starting note and the type of scale, for example, *A* major or *C* minor. The key is tonic, or the home tone for the musical piece. Your key and interval pattern (major or minor among others) provide all of the information you need as a vocalist to dive into practicing and working with scales.

So, if a song is in the key of *A* major, the pitches that will sound good in the song come from the *A*-major scale (*A*, *B*, *C♯*, *D*, *E*, *F*, *G♯*). Basically, the key tells you what notes you will be singing in a particular piece of music. And telling another musician that the piece is in *A* major is a lot cleaner than telling another musician, "We will be using the notes *A*, *B*, *C♯*, *D*, *E*, *F*, and *G♯*."

WHAT IS THE DIFFERENCE BETWEEN KEY AND PITCH?

Pitch is any note that you are matching. Key is a specific set of notes. For example, in the key of *C* major you have the notes *C*, *D*, *E*, *F*, *G*, *A*, and *B*. This follows the W W H W W W H pattern from above. To sing within the scale, you match the appropriate pitches. You move your voice to sing the notes and between those notes. If you swoop up to *C* (in other words, sliding your voice between notes), you may start your swoop at *B*, *E*, or some other note within the key. Our ears don't like it when we hit notes outside of the key, and that can make our singing sound unpleasant. Learning to stay on pitches/notes in the key and moving smoothly between them will determine, in part, how good your voice sounds. That's why it's important to practice scales, so you can internalize the sound of the notes in any particular key.

HOW MANY SINGING KEYS ARE THERE?

There are twelve keys in western music, from C, C♯/D♭, D, D♯/E♭, E, F, F♯/ G♭, G, G♯/A♭, A, A♯/B♭, B. The symbol that looks like a hash tag means sharp, and the symbol that looks like a *b* means flat. If you look at a piano keyboard, C♯ and D♭ are the same notes. The only difference is that one goes higher in pitch (sharp or ♯) and the other lower in pitch (flat or ♭). Remember you have different octaves as well (see Chapter 1), so if you are moving up the scale, the sharp symbol is used. If you move down the scale, the flat symbol is used. In terms of octaves, C3 and C4 are the same note, but C4 is vibrating twice as fast as C3.

The key describes the notes, and the type of scale describes the music's flavor. For example, *C* major and *C* minor sound different and have different notes, but both start with *C*. *A* minor and *C* major have the same notes, but sound different in application because when you use them the intervals you are using sound different because your ear hears the home note (*C* for *C* major and *A* for *A* minor). Check this out—get ready to blow your mind . . .

C major notes: *C D E F G A B*

A minor notes: *A B C D E F G*

The reason the same notes can sound different is based on the chords used in the scale and how they are used in a song. For example, in a lot of pop songs, especially older pop songs, the root note and the fourth and fifth note in the scale are used for the chord progression. For example, in *C* major this would be *C, F,* and *G.* In *A* minor this would be *A, D,* and *E.* In *A* minor this would be *A, D,* and *E.* If you write a song in *A* minor and it only uses the chords *C, F,* and *G,* you are really playing a *C* major song.

It's the way our ears hear it, so we describe it that way. Remember music theory, or your Map to Musical Freedom, is not rules but a description of how we hear sounds!

HOW DO I KNOW WHAT KEY A SONG IS IN?

You can determine this by where the song rests or comes back to home base. When you are listening, it's like you say, "ahhh, we're back at home." It is readily apparent by looking at the chords that the song contains. For example, if a song has a *C* major chord, *D* minor chord, *G* major chord, and an *A* minor chord, then it is either in *A* minor or *C* major and where the song rests—sounds like home—will determine which key it is in

Determining the key of a song as a beginner is difficult. But as you become more familiar with scales and their corresponding chords, you will be able to tell one key from another. Don't give up! It takes time, practice, and study, but you can do it.

HOW DO YOU CHANGE A SONG'S KEY?

If you maintain the same scale (i.e., distances between notes) and change the starting note, for example from *C* major to *D* major, you need to move each note up by a whole step (also called a major second). This is easy to do on a guitar as it literally means, for the most part, that you just slide up two frets. On a piano, this is more complicated, but the good news is that, for the vocalist, this is easier. Unless you are changing the key to something that is out of your **range** or has a lot of work around your **passaggio**, you literally just sing each note higher or lower depending on if you are raising or lowering the key.

So many beginning vocalists feel it is cheating to change the key of a song from the original to make it easier to sing. It's not! In fact, you owe it to yourself and the audience to sing in keys in which you are competent. And often, you don't have to change it very much. It could be you only need to go a half step above or below.

HOW DO I FIND THE BEST KEY FOR MY VOICE?

The best key for your voice will be determined by the song and the movement within the song. If you have problems managing your **vocal break** (also known as **passaggio)**, then you don't want a lot of notes or a melody that is focused right around your break. That is one of the reasons it's important to know where your break is. You also don't want to be straining to sing notes that are too high or low for you.

Follow these two steps: 1) Is the song within your range? If yes, move to step 2. If not, move the key up or down to match your range. In other words, are you straining to hit notes? Does your voice crack? 2) Do you have problems with the current key because the song melody is dancing around the few notes that are around your passaggio? If so, move the key up or down a half step in either direction. One of Jeff's professors from Berklee College of Music had this saying on her wall: "Salvation is only a half step away." You can move one whole to one and a half steps without really changing the character of the song. Try this and decide where the timbre of your voice (quality of the sound) is best. Where is the resonance the best? Where you can you most easily **belt** or use **mixed voice**? There are backing-track services that allow you to easily adjust the key to a song, and YouTube has increasing numbers of tracks of popular songs that are raised or lowered in key. Try it out!

WHAT IS AN EXERCISE THAT CAN HELP ME LEARN ABOUT KEYS?

Go to KaraokeVersion.com. (Please note: We are not affiliated with Karaoke Version, but use it in our studio.) Pick a song you can sing or a song you'd like to sing, then download the instrumental track in the original key, up one step and another two steps up, then one down a step and another two steps down. Sing all five versions (original, + 2 up, + 2 down). Which one is easiest? Which one is hardest? Do you need to go up more? Or down more? Try going three steps up or three steps down. Find your key!

CHAPTER 10

VOCAL HEALTH: TAKING GOOD CARE OF YOUR SINGING VOICE

W e are lucky to have the opportunity to lead a rock 'n roll singing group of about fifteen older people who range in age from sixties to mid-nineties, called the Forever Young Singers. One of the lovely women in the group has serious lung problems. When she first joined the group several months ago, she was on oxygen during the day. Her doctor learned of her love for singing and recommended that she sing to help to strengthen and increase her lung capacity. After only a few months of daily, but brief, vocal workouts (approximately fifteen minutes) and weekly group singing rehearsals, she no longer needs oxygen during the day and is working toward being able to go without it at night. We thought it was awesome that a doctor prescribed singing to improve her health!

IS SINGING GOOD FOR YOUR HEALTH?

Researchers have consistently found that singing is good for your health. Science has found that singing reduces the stress hormone, cortisol, in the body; can increase endorphins in your brain which promotes positive feelings; improves lung function; increases the hormone oxytocin, also known as the love hormone; and can enhance memory in people with dementia. That summarizes just a small amount of the evidence that says that singing produces great health benefits.

Singing is also good for mental health. When we sing, we tend to feel more connected to others, less depressed, and more upbeat. There is definite truth in that. When either one of us is feeling blue, all we have to do is participate in one of our singing classes! One study found that singers reported improvements in mental health, mood, and sense of well-being after participating in singing workshops. We could go on and on about how good singing is for you physically and mentally, so suffice it to say, you've picked a pursuit that is really good for you!

WHAT IS VOCAL HEALTH?

Vocal health is the overall functioning and health of the vocal folds, associated musculature, and tissues of the throat, as well as breathing capacity and control (which increases overall health). Taking care of your voice is called vocal hygiene. Later in this chapter, we will cover some tips to improve your vocal hygiene.

Sometimes overlooked, but important in singing, is care of your teeth. Good dental health is an indicator for overall health. Check in with your dentist to make sure your mouth is healthy. A healthy mouth is important because of its role in singing articulation involving the tongue, lips, cheeks, and throat.

HOW DO YOU KNOW IF YOUR VOICE ISN'T HEALTHY?

Any pain is cause for concern. If you feel pain when singing, see your primary care physician, who may need to refer you to an ear, nose, and throat specialist. Your primary doctor can diagnose many issues like allergies, colds, or other health concerns that can affect the voice. If you still feel pain or difficulty in using your voice, see an ear, nose, and throat physician with specialty in voice, if there is one in your area. This can be expensive, but your voice is your instrument that you will have your entire life, so you need to make sure it works properly.

Many people are worried when they choke or cough when trying to sing high notes. Most of the time this isn't cause for concern, but if you suspect a medical problem, see a doctor. It's better to be safe than sorry. Usually coughing, choking, or losing your voice when moving through your break or singing high notes results from pushing. This comes from engaging and overusing muscles other than those needed to engage the **CT or TA muscles** or trying to **belt** without proper training. This is quite common in beginning vocalists, but, with the right training, you can learn how to hit those notes without choking.

Work on relaxing as you sing. Check for tension in your shoulders and neck. Be aware of how tension feels, as well as the sensations associated with relaxation. Use **lip rolls** and a **chromatic scale** that take you right through your **chest voice, break**, and **head voice**. This will relax and reset your vocal folds if they aren't already too irritated. Get in the habit of using lip rolls for warmups and warm downs, although they do look and sound ridiculous!

HOW DO I WARMUP BEFORE SINGING?

It is vital that you warmup before you begin working out or singing songs. Warming up relaxes the muscles and vocal apparatus used in singing. We warmup using lip rolls in our studio. We've found they are effective in reducing discomfort and injury when working out or singing songs, particularly songs that involve belting, other strenuous vocal effects, and hitting notes at the upper end of your range. There are other exercises that you can add to your warmup such as stretching the neck and shoulders to produce relaxation, singing certain **intervals,** among others. But for beginners, start with lip rolls (also called lip trills) and then add other exercises over time as you develop your workout routine.

For those not familiar with lip rolls, they help to stretch out the vocal folds and warmup the muscles of your pharynx, mouth, cheeks, lips, and breathing apparatus. The lip roll is also effective is helping you learn to meter your breath. To do a lip roll, think of a little kid making the sound of an engine. Use the sound brrrr and make sure the vibration is occurring on your lips. When children make these engine sounds, they also vary the pitch, high notes for fast and lower notes for slow. These lip vibrations happen by the air passing through the lips. For many people, doing lip rolls is not easy. It took Jeff three months to master the exercise.

If you are having problems with lip rolls, don't give up. If you can't do it at first, it's probably because there is too much tension in your cheeks and jaw. Focus on relaxing those muscles. Second, your difficulty could come from not enough air being pushed through the lips. Here's a tip: gently place your fingers on the sides of your jaw to push your cheeks up. Puff out your lips and relax your cheeks. Then exhale with a controlled stream of air through your lips. Experiment with the force of the exhalation and see what works. We promise you will eventually get it!

Warmup by doing lip rolls to a chromatic scale. A chromatic scale and demonstration of lip rolls can be found on our website.

WHAT CAUSES VOICE PROBLEMS?

The good news is that most voice problems are caused by overuse and straining of the voice, like yelling or screaming, loud talking, singing without warming up, pushing while singing, excessive throat clearing, and coughing, to name a few. An analogy is clapping your hands. If you clap your hands softly, your hands don't hurt. But if you clap them hard, they start to tingle and then become irritated. If you kept on clapping, you might get blisters on your hands. Screaming, coughing, and talking loudly or excessively can all slam the vocal folds together, causing injury. Most of these things are under your control, which means you can avoid voice problems by staying hydrated, practicing good overall health habits, and learning proper singing and speaking technique.

If you have concern about what is causing any voice problems you may have, visit a doctor. While you can rehabilitate your voice and take care of it so it is in the best shape possible, you want to rule out nodules, tears, and other physical issues with your voice before you self-diagnose. Your voice is important, so take the time to see a specialist, then engage a coach with experience in voice rehabilitation if you suspect you have voice damage.

Here are some major don'ts:

- Never sing through pain.

- Never sing after you lose your voice.

- Stop singing if you start to cough or choke when singing particular passages.

- Avoid talking loudly for extended periods of time.

- Avoid vigorous throat clearing. Instead, dry swallow, take small sips of water, laugh gently then swallow, or hum lightly. You can also use a gentle throat clear without forcing the breath. It sounds like a small puff of air produced in the throat. Some people clear their throat unconsciously, so it may take some time to become aware of this habit.

- Don't push or strain—use peripheral muscles to sing (you cough or choke when this happens).

- Don't belt your way through a song because you can't move between degrees of mixed voice.

WHAT ARE THE BEST WAYS TO CARE FOR MY SINGING VOICE?

There are many things you can do to care for your singing voice. Here is what we advise our students to do:

- Always warmup before you sing. Use lip rolls and a chromatic scale for at least two to three minutes.

- Stay hydrated.

- Eat a well-balanced diet and get appropriate rest.

- If you have concerns about your voice, get your voice apparatus assessed by a qualified physician.

- Always warmup with lip trills before singing.

- Learn how to navigate your break in a relaxed and controlled way.

- Learn how to use mixed voice and belt the right way. If you are straining when belting, then you aren't doing it correctly.

- Never grind your vocal folds. There are safe ways to produce singing effects such as growling.

- Avoid glottal stops (slamming the vocal folds together—you hear a slight pop as you start singing). Glottal stops can occur when we sing consonants, especially at the onset of singing.

- Do singing workouts daily in the right way (see exercises on our website to get you started).

- Find your **range** and expand it in a healthy way.

- Consult an expert coach if you have any questions about the above.

These are all great tips to follow to care for your voice, but we would be remiss if we didn't address the importance of your attitude and outlook on your singing and voice care. Improving your singing is like going to a gym. You don't improve your physical performance overnight; it takes consistent and proper workouts for you to eventually see results. In terms of your singing, give yourself a full six months to improve and commit to fifteen minutes per day at least five days a week to improve your voice. If you miss a day, resume your practice the next day. If singing is truly important to you, finding fifteen minutes per day five days a week (that's only an hour and fifteen minutes per week!) should not be a problem. You'll find this is enough to get you to the next level in most cases. If you aren't seeing results, engage a qualified coach to check your approach to working out.

When you are done with your exercises each day, reward yourself by singing songs that you like. Don't get sucked into a YouTube singing wormhole where you're looking for the secret to great singing instead of working out your voice. You will lose hours in trying to find a shortcut to getting your voice in shape. The shortcut is actually working out and not watching videos—take the fifteen minutes and do it! And don't fall for supplements that promise improvement in your singing. Nothing substitutes for putting in those fifteen minutes daily.

Be careful of what you say to yourself. Never say, "I suck" or "My voice is terrible." Recognize that the voice is a dynamic organism that requires daily work to improve. What good comes from this type of self-talk? Nothing. Tell yourself that you are committed to your singing and that with each workout, you are getting better. While you may not be the singer you want to be right now, realize that you are better at it than when you first started, and if you keep working, you'll only improve.

Decide when you are going to sing each day and develop a habit. If you know when you are going to sing (for example, during your lunch break in the car), you don't have to think about, *When am I going to get my workout in today?* It's set. No additional mental energy needed!

In summary, the best way to care for our voices and improve them the fastest way possible is:

1. Warmup before you work out or sing;

2. Hydrate;

3. Eat a well-balanced diet most of the time;

4. Keep a positive mental attitude.

CHAPTER 11

PERFORMANCE: SHARING YOUR VOICE WITH OTHERS

Sometimes we get prospective students in our studio who say to us, "I really just want to sing for myself. I'm not interested in being a rock star." Almost all aspiring vocalists have a drive to perform, and a few are afraid to say it out loud. Working hard to improve your singing can be reinforcing by itself, but most singers have something they want to communicate with others through song. We love it when someone comes in and says, "I want to be a pro performer!" Stating who you want to be gets you there faster than hiding your aspirations. In fact, hiding your dreams will hold you back!

While we acknowledge there are different types of performances, for example, recording performances, social media videos, and others, this chapter is focused on live performing which the majority of our students are interested in. For some, live performances can be as anxiety provoking as they are rewarding, so this chapter answers questions that can help increase your knowledge about performing and hopefully take away some of that trepidation.

WHAT MAKES A GOOD SINGING PERFORMANCE?

A good singing performance communicates to the audience the emotion intended by the performer. Sometimes, however, the emotion communicated isn't exactly what the performer wanted to evoke—some performances may have varying emotional impacts on different audience members. Performers need to ask themselves, *What emotion am I trying to convey in this particular song? Is it longing? Sadness? Joy? And once the message is determined, how can I best communicate this?*

Vocalists communicate emotion not only through singing but also through visual means including body movement, utilization of the stage space, and making eye contact with the audience. Communicating emotion as a performer can make you feel vulnerable and even exposed. We can feel funny communicating that raw energy and emotion to strangers (or even more so to people we know and love!). We don't want to embarrass ourselves, so we might underplay our performance. When you do this, you undermine your potential best performance out of fear. Regardless of your level, the audience will sense your hesitation and your performance will be less than it could be.

Think about the great vocalists you have seen perform. What qualities do they possess? We bet that a great technical performance doesn't come to mind first. Most likely, you remember performers who put their heart and soul into the performance. In fact, technically superior vocal performances that lack other components such as expressive movement can be inferior overall to performances that leave it all on the floor. As Fred Astaire said, "Do it big, do it right, and do it with style."

Far less common is when people use whatever emotion they feel at the time to guide their performance. On occasion we get performers who say, "I need the audience's energy to drive me. I feed off that energy to drive my performance." While this may be partly true, this creates two problems. First, if the audience is lackluster or not warmed up yet, your performance will match that if you are using the audience's energy as a driver. Second, you really have no control over your performance since you are counting on the audience to drive your performance. Don't do this! Create the performance you want, and give that gift to the audience.

As a performer you have a responsibility to communicate, educate, and entertain, depending on the venue and performance. The audience may not be the most receptive or enthusiastic, but you can have the ability through a great performance to transform the audience. Great vocal performances inspire, motivate, educate, and persuade. To have this sort of impact, you've got to treat the performance itself as important and not rely solely on vocal technique. Give equal time to performance and technique, and you will really shine as a performer.

HOW CAN I BEST PREPARE FOR A SINGING PERFORMANCE?

One word: rehearsing. You must practice—that is, your technical vocal factors, performance metrics (how you look and move on stage), and how the two work together to create the energy and emotion you are working to convey. You should start practicing in front of a mirror so you can see what you look like when performing. If this isn't practical, video yourself. What performance factors match what you are trying to convey? What factors take away from your performance? Make a list corresponding to each category, rehearse, and then video yourself again. Work toward the performance that you can be proud of, one that expresses your own unique style.

With our students, we always include mental work, such as affirmations, aspirations, meditation, and mindfulness as part of the process. Muscle tension and/or negative thoughts during (or before!) a show can seriously detract from your performance. Focusing on the past or the future during your performance can negatively impact your show. Rehearse focusing on the now—this is the note I'm singing and the next note I'm going to sing. If you prepare that way, your performance will shine.

WHAT SHOULD I DO ON STAGE WHEN SINGING?

If you are anxious before a performance, you want to calm your body down. Anxiety manifests itself both physically and cognitively. Take a few moments before you go on stage and do some breath work. Slowly take deep breaths in and release them in a controlled manner. You can also use the square-breathing technique. Here are the steps:

1. begin by slowly exhaling all of your air out;

2. slowly inhale through your nose to a slow count of four;

3. hold at the top of the breath for a count of four;

4. slowly exhale through your mouth for a count of four;

5. at the bottom of the breath, pause and hold for a count of four.

Think about this as a square with each inhalation, exhalation and pause as the sides of the square.

Once you are on stage, stand up straight while being relaxed. Keep your feet about shoulder-width apart with one foot ever so slightly in front of the other to give you a strong base. Smile at the audience. Breathe regularly. If making eye contact causes you stress, focus on people's foreheads or the back of the room just above eye level. Focus intently on the music you will be singing, not what you think the audience thinks about the music you are singing!

Make sure you use your microphone as part of your dynamics. Closer to your mouth is louder, or it can be more intimate if you are singing softly. If you're going to start singing loudly, move your microphone away so the audience isn't deafened by the change in volume. Focus on the sound the audience hears through the speakers and not the sound of your unamplified voice unless it's a small venue, and you're not using a microphone. We recommend that you practice your songs with a microphone and amplifier if you are going to perform using one. How you use the microphone is part of your singing performance, and you should practice using it just like you practice singing your songs.

Relax your hands and arms and gesture in a way that adds to your performances. Don't put your hands in your pockets or cross your arms. You want to be a dynamic presence, not a stiff board on stage! Don't try and cross your legs, as this may increase the chance that you will trip and fall down. And if you do happen to fall, just keep singing!

If you are singing with a band (or even to backing tracks), watch the floor for cords and other obstructions that can trip you. The more instruments on stage, the more trip hazards. If you have a sound check, make sure you know where the cords are going to be, and if possible, work with your band mates to tape down cords that will not move during the performance. Make sure you know where the stage ends so you don't fall off. While there are parts of songs you may sing with your eyes closed for emotional impact, use this technique strategically and don't sing the entire time with your eyes closed. Don't look at the floor.

Treat all parts of the audience as equally important—sing to the sides of the venue as well as the center. This tip came directly from an audience member during one of our performances who felt left out because Crystal kept looking the center of the auditorium and not the sides. Sometimes we have the tendency to want to focus on the part of the audience that is most reinforcing – those people who are looking at you, nodding their heads in rhythm, or seem to be more engaged with the music than other parts of the audience who aren't as enthusiastic. Focus on the other segments of the audience that may seem less engaged, so they have a chance to connect with you as you perform.

Finally, make your performances about the music, not about what you think the audience thinks about you or your performance. (Did you follow that?!) You're there to entertain, and if you focus on the music and the message you are trying to convey, you won't have as much of an opportunity to worry if the guy in row six likes you or not!

WHAT ARE STRATEGIES TO MEMORIZE LYRICS?

One strategy is to focus on visual imagery when you are memorizing lyrics. For example, the first line of Journey's "Don't Stop Believin'" is "Just a small town girl." Think of a miniature girl standing on the street corner of a toy-sized town and waving at you. This kind of crazy imagery really works to cement the lyrics at the first level. Pick a song and discover what type of visual imagery works for you.

When you memorize lyrics, try to memorize the lyrics in chunks rather than starting at the beginning and working on memorization from the very beginning. Chunks could include each verse separately, the chorus, and, if the song has one, the bridge. Why is this important? When people try to memorize lyrics from the very beginning and start at the beginning each time they work on memorization, you end up knowing the first verse super well (because you've repeated it so many times), and the other verses less well—especially that last verse.

Have you ever been singing and forget a line? Believe us, if you perform enough, it will happen. It happens to everyone, including the pros! But you can recover, especially if you have memorized the lyrics in chunks. If you memorize from the very beginning, it is more difficult to resume where you are in the song. For example, if you flub a line in verse two, it's easier for you to jump back on the horse (so to speak) because you aren't using all that mental bandwidth to try to remember the song from the very beginning.

A third method is to focus on vowel sounds and melody. This is a superior method, but it requires more practice and experience—possibly one to two years of experience routinely singing songs from memory. Using the Journey example cited above, the vowel break down would be:

Just a small town girl = y+uh+s T+uh+sm+ah+ll+t+how+n G+uh+r+el

Learn more about singing vowels in Chapter 8.

Finally, avoid practicing by singing with the original artist or using karaoke software or a machine. You may need to do this initially to learn the song, its timing, and its nuances, but doing this long term is a crutch. We always sound better when we sing with the artist (we nail it in the car, right?) and karaoke tells us what to sing when. But sometimes the timing presented in karaoke is wrong, or you want to use a little different timing to make the song your own. Once you have the song basics down, only sing with an instrumental backing track and wean yourself off printed lyrics as quickly as possible. In our studio, we often use the custom backing tracks from karaoke-version.com/custombackingtrack/. They tend to good quality and are about $3 for each track. (We are not financially affiliated with this service, and there are lots of other services to choose from.)

WHAT KIND OF EQUIPMENT DO I NEED AS A VOCALIST?

The minimum equipment you need is yourself (well nourished, hydrated, and healthy!), a water bottle, a binder for lead sheets or lyrics, a microphone, a small PA with effects, and headphones. You should practice as your audience will hear you, not like it sounds when you sing in the shower or acapella as you walk your dog. This is why you want to invest in a small PA with vocal effects and a dynamic microphone. At this writing, a small starter PA with effects can run about $300 to $500, but is well worth the investment. You can also get a dynamic microphone, a microphone stand, and a cable for about $150. This investment is much less than what most other musicians spend, as they need to purchase their instrument in addition to amplification devices. A keyboard is also important to map melodies and check your pitch ($50 to $500), as is software to verify your pitch and analyze your voice ($10 to $300 depending on the metrics that the software analyzes).

You also want a professional-looking bag to organize your equipment. Make sure everything is carefully stored and ready to use. You don't want to fumble around untwisting your cord or searching for your mic!

It's likely that you'll be showing up to auditions or band practice with this equipment. Do not assume that a venue has equipment for you. Even if the band you're playing with has a PA, you can use your small PA as a monitor for your singing. A monitor is a performer-facing speaker that allows you to hear your own singing. (They are also called stage monitors, floor monitors, or wedges.) If you arrive at your audition and they have equipment, no worries – you will look like a serious pro!

Music is an expression of the soul; it's art—always. But, when tickets are for sale, it's a business, pure and simple. The venue owner or manager of the group may be a big music fan, but if they've been in business for a while, they've been burned by flaky musicians—don't add to their burden. If you are well rehearsed and professional, you may end up a star—just because you showed up with the right equipment on time.

HOW DO I OVERCOME PERFORMANCE ANXIETY/ STAGE FRIGHT AS A SINGER?

Have you ever felt butterflies in your stomach before you sing in front of an audience? Started sweating? Worried that someone will judge your singing like Simon Cowell judges singing contestants? You're not alone. Depending on the study you read, between 17 percent and a whopping 60 percent of musicians experience stage fright (also called performance anxiety).

Stage fright has several different symptoms, and how each person experiences these symptoms is unique. Some singers have emotional reactions like fear, dread, or worry about being judged harshly. Fear and anxiety can get in the way of you hitting those awesome high notes because your vocal apparatus and other muscles in your body tighten up. These emotions are often fueled by thoughts including perfectionism and harsh self-talk. This can lead to physiological responses such as racing heart, butterflies in the stomach, sweating, and dry mouth (which is horrible for vocalists). These symptoms are all interrelated—thoughts of being judged harshly leads to fear, which can cause a pit in the stomach and muscle tension that affect your ability to do that awesome run. Then your performance suffers, and your fears get worse—it's a vicious cycle!

One of the things you need to understand is how the body responds to stress. The part of your nervous system that controls the fight-or-flight reaction is responsible for the body symptoms you experience. Way back when humans faced real dangers—saber tooth tigers lurking around the corner, the neighboring clan of cave people coming to beat the snot out of you—the body jacked itself up to either run like hell or kick some butt. Unfortunately, that reaction really isn't helpful in most stressful situations that modern humans face. So what's a singer to do?

The first step is awareness: Become aware of tension in your body when you're going to perform or just thinking about performing. Sing and imagine you are in front of 500 people. See them. Feel the heat of the lights. Really visualize the details of the scene. Now notice where you are tightening up.

Once you know how your body responds and where you hold your stress reactions, use visualization again. In a quiet place, take a few deep breaths and imagine you are singing in front of those 500 people while focusing on relaxing the part of your body that tightens up. See yourself relaxed and singing the song just like you want to. Immerse yourself in the scene and notice details. Visualization is a proven technique among athletes, so even though it may seem hokey to you, give it a shot for a week to see how it works. You might be surprised!

If you're at the venue and anxiety starts to creep in, use the square breathing technique (covered in Chapter 11). This will calm your body and mind—know that anxiety and relaxation are incompatible responses. In other words, you can't be relaxed and anxious at the same time, so let's go for relaxation. You can help to accomplish this through square breathing.

One of the biggest causes of performance anxiety is your thoughts.

- I'm not as good as so-and-so singer.

- People aren't going to like my voice.

- What if I forget the words or when to come in?

Do any of these sound familiar? So we ask you this question: Does anything good come from you thinking that way? No! The first step in changing these self-sabotaging thoughts is noticing them. Most people aren't aware of the critical monologue going on in their heads, so when you feel your body reacting, pay attention to what you are thinking at that time. Write those thoughts down and then write down facts that challenge those thoughts. Consult your singing coach or a trusted friend to help you come up with facts that challenge your negative thought patterns.

Finally, try reframing the anxiety. Is it stage fright, or could it be excitement to perform? Say to yourself (and work on believing it), *I'm super excited to perform! This is what I've worked so hard for. It'll be fun!* You'll have to repeat this over and over, but you can change how you think about the body reactions you are having before performing.

Battling performance anxiety is a process, so be patient. And the goal isn't to get rid of all the anxiety. Some of that energy can be used to motivate you to do your best and to keep practicing! Try these and other strategies to get your anxiety working for you instead of against you.

Finally, here's the kicker: the best way to overcome fear about singing in front of people is to do just that—sing in front of people! Make sure you start performing often and early, beginning with small, friendly groups. At our studio, we recommend small group lessons from the beginning for most vocalists so that they can begin to perform in front of others on a regular basis. Learning how to interact with a group and deal with anxiety is one of your biggest and important challenges. Give the suggestions above a try. You can do it!

HOW DO I BEST WORK WITH OTHER MUSICIANS?

The best way to work with other musicians is very similar to how you work with hiring managers, producers, and venue owners: show up on time, be ready to perform, and focus on the music. Keep telling yourself, *It's all about the music!*

If you are in another person's studio, don't start hooking up equipment or performing unless invited to. Most musicians don't care, but it's like going to another person's house, walking to the refrigerator, and helping yourself to food—many won't care, but it is important to ask first.

Behave like a serious musician—be polite, professional, and focused. And above all, listen! Think of music as a conversation. Most people, or most non-annoying people, don't sit down and start lecturing people on random topics. They ask questions, respond, and interact. It is the same when you add music. Sometimes at a heavy metal jam, it can be deafeningly loud, but if you are dealing with pros, it can be very interactive and polite as well. Don't assume that your behavior should be governed based on a YouTube video you've seen or the stories your uncle Charlie talked about when he was in a band.

With the above said, don't let others put you down and determine what you do. While it is always important to be open to constructive criticism, you've got to assess whether the feedback is appropriate and helpful for you (with the emphasis on helpful). Speak up for yourself, and if it isn't the right group, work on finding another group. Your voice deserves to be heard. We have found that that the higher up the ladder you go as a vocalist, the easier it is to work with people. When you get out of the garage and bar-band scene and start to work with higher-level musicians, most are respectful and professional (of course, there are exceptions). If you want to progress, surround yourself with serious people and ditch the negative self-talk. You deserve to be there performing!

HOW DO I FIND OPPORTUNITIES TO PERFORM?

Finally, we want to give you some ideas to get you started performing in your local area. Opportunities to perform are everywhere, and once you have a few songs you can confidently sing under your belt, you should perform whenever you get the chance. Here are some tried and true ways to find performance venues.

1. Don't hold people hostage but ask friends and family to listen to a live musical piece once and while.

2. Offer to play a few songs at a house party.

3. Sing at your next gathering of close friends.

4. Attend open mic performances—remember to ask what equipment they have and what you need to bring.

5. After you've built your confidence through playing some small public performances, ask local bars if you could open for their paid acts for free. Share your setlist and be specific about what you can do for them. Don't undersell or oversell your services, it's just an opportunity for them to have some music for free during a possible dead period for live performances.

6. Approach your local library and ask if you could perform.

7. Scour your local music store's bulletin board or other places where local musicians place ads. This can be a great opportunity to collaborate. Respond to ads or put up a poster asking for local musicians who want to perform in your genre.

8. Advertise singing for weddings for free—however, remember to have a set list that you can perform and have a quality recording of your work.

Don't be afraid to approach larger venues when you have ten to twenty songs. Does the local music arena need a free act to warmup before a concert? Does your local fair need acts? Does the local farmer's market need music? Contact music promoters in your area and see if there are opportunities to perform at your skill level. If you have one song you can perform well, that is a great start. If you have three, it's time to get out there. If you have ten or fifteen and you're not performing, you're holding back your progress. Get out of the basement or your bedroom, and share you voice with the world. It's a great gift to give others.

CHAPTER 12

TOOLS TO HELP YOU ON YOUR SINGING JOURNEY

This chapter isn't in our typical question-and-answer format. Instead, we'll be sharing some tips that bring the content from the previous chapters together to help you get on the road to success as a vocalist. While good technique is always important in singing, there are many other aspects you should consider if you are thinking about singing as a possible career or even a serious avocation.

MAKE A PLAN AND STICK TO IT

Let's consider your singing future: The most important thing you can do is focus on the present and the future. If we focus on the past, it's only to glean lessons from what we've done. The most important time is what is happening now and where you are going in the future. Here are the vital questions:

1. Where are you now?

2. Where do you want to go?

Once you figure that out, your next step is to find a reasonable path from point number one to point number two. This may be a daunting task, but deciding where you want to go can crystalize your thinking and give you the motivation to keep pushing forward. This is one of the most critical pieces of a performance musician's training, and one of the most neglected. If you don't decide where you want to go, you could waste time acquiring skills you don't need and miss getting the skills that you do need.

For example, Elizabeth's goal is to up her singing game and become a serious vocalist. She's heard good things about Berklee College of Music, so she spends the next four years studying voice at that prestigious institution of higher learning. She reads all kinds of books about voice and learns how to sight read staff. When she graduates, she says, "I want to start working as a vocalist." Her goal of graduating from Berklee is certainly laudable, but during her time there she really didn't think very deeply about what type of working vocalist she wanted to be. *Working in what way? With whom? How do I want to make money as a singer? Do I want to be a performer? A teacher? A studio musician?* Elizabeth's accomplishment is certainly impressive, but she didn't plan beyond graduation.

In that same amount of time, Elizabeth could have acquired the necessary skills to be a performing vocalist (let's assume that was her goal), have a press kit, three to four years of performing experience (including collaborating with other musicians), and have two CDs worth of her own music streaming on all of the services as well as featured on her performance website. She could have contacted agents, spent time singing at small venues, backing up other singers, and could have steady gigs four nights a week. We're not saying that getting a Berklee education isn't worthwhile (both of us studied there), but a person should ask themselves, *How does this fit in with my ultimate goal?*

In the first scenario, Elizabeth thoroughly learned the technical pieces of singing (which, again, is impressive). In the second scenario, she planned a career. And of course, those two paths aren't mutually exclusive.

One could be enrolled at Berklee or some other prestigious music school and successfully plan for a future of performing. The point is this: know where you want to end up and take the necessary steps to increase the likelihood you'll get there. Of course, circumstances change, which force changes in plans. (Isn't there an old saying, "We plan and God laughs?") So, you need flexibility to be able to pivot when absolutely necessary. On the other hand, hard times come and go, and if we can stay true to our dreams and consistent with executing our plans, we are much, much more likely to be successful.

In the next section, we talk about some tried-and-true methods that will help you stay on the path of being the type of musician you want to be.

KEEPING A MUSIC JOURNAL

We strongly encourage our vocalists to have a central place where they can track their short- and long-term goals, their practice sessions, what was done during practice, how they felt during practice, singing metrics (covered later in this chapter), music they'd like to work on, cool songs they've heard, and successes and difficulties experienced along the way. We know that is quite a bit to document, so starting off small and using your journal to write down your goals and when you practice is a great start.

Journaling can be done in hard copy or digitally; do whatever works for you so you're more likely to keep a journal. If it's in hardcopy form, pick out a journal that is appealing to you. Chronicling your practice and other topics related to your singing is a form of accountability. You know you will be documenting what you are doing to keep a record. You can then use what you've written to reflect on your goals and the journey you are taking to meet those goals. Using a music journal can be a great tool when you are working with a voice coach or voice instructor.

CHOOSING AND WORKING WITH A VOICE COACH

If your ambition is to become the best vocalist you can be, you should engage the services of a good (if not great) voice coach. Can you do it without one? Yes, but it is much more difficult and slower. Singing is much more than information. Singing is applying the right exercises and information to your voice—there is no one-size-fits-all training program. If you see a training program that says this is for every singer, then you know it isn't targeted to you. You should have exercises that match your **head voice** range, **chest voice** range, and **break** range.

Much of the information that is needed to learn about singing (and music in general) is available from many different sources, including books (like this one!), instructional videos, and, of course, the Internet. Even though a lot of information is readily available, some of it's incorrect, incomplete, and otherwise bad information (this is especially true for a lot of information found on the Internet!). That is one of the reasons we wrote this book. Through our many years of experience coaching and teaching musicians, coupled with the knowledge we have gained through formal education and from the teachers we have had the privilege to work with, we've sifted through the good, bad, and ugly information found on the Internet to provide you with evidence-based answers to your singing questions.

But our book—or any book—isn't going to be enough to accomplish your goals, particularly if you want to be a professional vocalist. You'll will need the guidance of an excellent teacher so you can fully understand and apply the correct information. The good news is if you just want to sing better, this book will be very helpful. Just like you wouldn't try to become a doctor by just reading a book, you will find it difficult to compete with other vocalists unless you get a vocal coach. YouTube and DVDs can provide you with exercises and information, but again, be careful about the quality of that information. They can't listen to your singing and point out the strengths on which you can build and any weaknesses you need to correct. From our perspective, there is no substitute for a competent voice coach listening to your singing and providing you with expert feedback and encouragement.

Great voice coaches provide you with supportive as well as corrective feedback. They build on your strengths and tell you what you need to do differently. Their advice is most often specific instead of general. A quality coach will provide feedback about both the training process and the performance outcome. In other words, they manage and schedule new materials and effectively explain their importance. They provide guidance as to how you should manage your practice time to get the biggest bang for your buck (or the best performance payoff in the shortest amount of time). In terms of outcome, a great coach should give you an unbiased assessment of a performance.

They help you to build up your confidence level (even if you are not consciously aware that this is happening). A great vocal coach will help you become secure with your technical skills so you can execute difficult vocal techniques comfortably. These teachers value creativity (e.g., improvising and songwriting) and performing. Awesome teachers want to make sure that you fully understand what you're learning and, most importantly, teach you how to apply it by giving you detailed explanations and encouraging you to ask questions when something is unclear. They sincerely care about your musical growth and development.

An experienced and competent teacher will take you far beyond what you could learn on your own because they address you as a unique singer, they just don't give you information and tell you to work on it. If you're stuck where you are as a vocalist, a good coach can get you unstuck. A poor coach will tell you to work harder or that you'll get it eventually—these types of coaches are ones that you should avoid. Your coach should ask you on occasion, "What is your biggest problem or concern?" And then, they should work with you to fix it.

This doesn't mean you have to engage with a teacher weekly for your whole vocal career. It can be quite expensive, but on the other hand, aren't your dreams worthy of a significant investment? Many vocalists work with a great coach on and off as they work toward perfecting their art. If money is an issue, try seeing a coach once a month. You can supplement this coaching with reputable books and other resources in between working with your coach. In our studio, many of our vocalists come in every other week, unless they're preparing for a big performance, which may prompt weekly sessions.

Unfortunately, anyone can claim to be a great voice teacher and there are many people who make this claim. The number of competent teachers, however, is limited. This brings us to this crucial issue: How can a student find, choose, and then accurately evaluate a singing coach?

Here are some questions that you should ask any voice teacher you're considering:

1. *What is your teaching experience? How were you trained in teaching?* Good teachers start by being trained to teach! Find out where they were trained to teach, and if they weren't trained to teach, then realize that they need an extra three to five years of experimenting on students to become good teachers.

2. *How long have you been teaching and approximately how many students have you taught during that time?* At least two to three years of teaching experience is preferred. You take a risk with a teacher who has been teaching less than one year unless they have been trained as an instructor. It's preferable that the teacher has taught a moderate to large number of students. It takes time for a teacher to really learn how to teach well, and the main way that someone learns to teach is by teaching! The teacher learns how to teach over time and will make some mistakes in the beginning of their career. You don't want to be one of those first thirty to fifty students where those mistakes are made. Let that teacher gain their experience by making mistakes on someone else.

3. *What styles of music do you teach best?* Make sure that you ask this question before telling the prospective teacher what style of music you want to learn. A lot of teachers claim to teach all styles of music well, but beware! Don't be impressed by someone who tells you that they can teach every style of music well. If you really want to be a rock vocalist you want to take lessons from a contemporary music teacher, not a classically trained teacher who claims to teach all styles well. Find yourself a good rock teacher. If you want to learn multiple styles of music that are not similar (like country, opera, and heavy metal) take lessons from different teachers for each of those styles. However, beginners should be less concerned with style until they master the basics of matching pitch, timing, movement in **head** and **chest** voice, and so on.

4. *What is the cost of lessons?* Excellent teachers are in demand and usually have a lot of students. These teachers often are not cheap. The going rate for good teachers in our area (Capital District in New York State) is between $35 and $75 per half-hour private lesson. Rates may be different in your state or country, and some teachers only teach in hour blocks which increases the price. There are a growing number of teachers online. Usually, these lessons are less expensive in the long run. But remember, you get what you pay for. While considering your budget is realistic and important for many people, if it's your primary factor in choosing a voice coach, you'll likely be disappointed. If you can't afford to pay the higher rates for a really good voice teacher, see if you can take lessons on a bi-weekly or even every three weeks instead of taking more-frequent lessons. Quality is more important than quantity in this arena.

5. *Can you tell me how you teach the lessons?* This is probably the most important question that you can ask a teacher. The answer to this question can really help you to determine if a teacher is competent, because this is a trick question. Anyone can tell you

that they have been teaching for 100 years and that they have had 10,000 students and the cost is $1,000 per lesson because they are the greatest teacher of all time, but an inexperienced teacher cannot fool you with his or her answer to this question (unless they are reading this chapter!). If a prospective teacher who doesn't know you, your musical knowledge, singing skill baseline, and/ or musical tastes and singing goals tries to explain how they will teach you, then this isn't a competent teacher. They need to know about you before they can tell you the content of your lessons and how they will be taught.

So, what would an experienced and competent teacher say to you when you ask the question? We explain to prospective students that a lesson plan can't be formulated for anyone until we learn a lot more about that student—who they are, what they want, their current skill level, and so on. We also do a voice assessment for prospective students before they sign up with our studio. We test pitch matching using technology for objectivity, aural skills, rhythm, and other singing metrics not as an audition, but to help us meet students where they are and provide them with some initial feedback. Once we do that, we discuss if our studio is a good fit. Not all teachers are appropriate for all students. Watch out for one who claims they are.

In addition to asking the questions above, here are some other things to consider.

- Just because a teacher may have some talented students (or stars they taught back in the day), that does not necessarily mean that the teacher is great. This might seem like a good criterion for evaluating a teacher, but sometimes students were already at a relatively advanced level before engaging with this voice coach.

- Some teachers tell their students to try to learn from as many sources as possible and then leave it up to you to sort through it all and decide what works best for you. How are you supposed to sift through all of that information? How is a student to know the best exercise to work with their break? To expand their range? This is one of the reasons why you have a teacher; it is their job to teach you these things, and this is why you are giving the teacher your money! If you were already an expert, you could be the teacher. As such, your voice coach should be solving your problems and not telling you to study more or work harder!

- Don't assume that someone is a good teacher just because they may be an excellent vocalist or have good credentials. We know plenty of competent singers with advanced music degrees who aren't good teachers. We also know some great musicians who are terrible teachers as they were never taught how to competently teach voice. We were fortunate to have some truly great teachers, but we've had some incompetent ones along the way, too.

The following factors aren't required for someone to be a great vocal coach, but it certainly is to your advantage to have a teacher who has these subjects as part of their knowledge base.

Voice pedagogy. This is knowing how to teach voice. There's a difference between knowing how to sing well and how to effectively teach you how to sing. Having a voice coach who's been trained in how to teach voice is critical. You will benefit greatly from a teacher who can teach you how to integrate a variety of techniques into your singing, including music theory, ear training, song writing, improvisation, and so on. But teaching voice isn't just about teaching techniques. A competent voice coach should also understand how to teach various learning styles and teach different personality types most effectively—not everyone learns the same way, and not everyone has the same needs. Every student is different, and each of those students may learn and comprehend information in different ways. It's important for any teacher to understand this. For example, we teach students with special needs in our studio, and adapt our teaching style to most effectively work with these individuals.

Recording advice. One of the best ways to help you progress is to record and listen to your singing with as unbiased ear as possible. The better you become as a musician, the more likely it will be that you'll want to record yourself. If you have little or no experience using software designed for musicians, having someone who can help guide you is especially helpful.

Music business. If you plan to record, release, and sell your own music now or in the future, there is a huge amount of music business information that is necessary to acquire if you want to make any money. Some teachers who have released their own album and are promoting it themselves can be a great source of help for selling your own work. (But that is not the only criterion!) You can also learn other things, like how to set up gigs for your band and how to get the press to write about you.

Finally, voice coaching is a service. You're paying someone to help you reach your goals. If you aren't comfortable with the coach, this can definitely impede your progress. If you don't look forward to lessons or aren't progressing even incrementally, don't be shy about telling a voice coach they aren't a good fit for you. If they're a pro, they'll understand that they're not suited to teach everyone. Remember, this is a service that you pay for—you're not paying to have a friend.

Getting a great vocal instructor may take some time, and we know you want to spend the money with the one who gets one who gets results. This is cheaper than saving a few dollars and going for years without progress. One session with a great vocal coach is worth more than a hundred with an average or poor coach. In fact, just like with every other profession, a poor coach can lead you astray and a good coach can point you in the right direction.

SINGING METRICS AND EVALUATING YOUR OWN SINGING

Even under the guidance of a skilled coach, it can be helpful for you to evaluate your own singing using objective metrics to help you see how you have progressed and what you may need to work on. The chart below presents a series of metrics that can help guide your workouts. Work on one metric along with other voice-strengthening exercises and performance skills. Once you can meet the metric's criterion, move to the next metric. That doesn't mean you don't go back and continue to work on the previous categories, you just spend a little more time in your workouts on the benchmark you are trying to meet. These metrics go from foundational to more advanced and are presented in that order.

You can go to our website to get basic exercises that cover each of these areas.

Metric	If answer is yes:	If answer is no:
Can you match pitch throughout your range?	Move to next metric	Focus on **chromatic** exercises for pitch matching.
Is your range at least two octaves up to at least *A4*?	Move to next metric	To increase your **range** safely, start with straw exercise (see website for explanation and demonstration). Focus on developing your **head voice** using a chromatic track which works your **CT muscle** group. Each day, move your starting note up one note for at least two weeks. Do not strain!

Can you hold a note on pitch for at least 10 seconds?	Move to next metric	Using a high-quality app and a timer, sing a note and hold it for as long as you can keeping the note on pitch.
Can you sing intervals m2, M2, m3, M3, P4, tritone, and P5?	Move to next metric	Sing intervals from a note that is comfortable for you. See the website for a practice track to help you train on intervals.
Can you sing harmony third and fifth?	Move to next metric	Work on harmonies using a practice track on the website. After you have mastered those exercises, find someone to sing with using a high-quality pitch detector to help you find the harmony notes.
Can you sing from your lowest note to your highest note, at least two octaves, smoothly navigating your break and without straining?	Move to next metric	Focus on semi-occluded consonants (such as /m/ or /n/) or straw exercise (both examples on the website) with chromatic scales to extend your range safely.
Can you sing a scale from a chosen note, for example, A3, B3, and C4 acapella?	Move to next metric	Find a starting note and sing the major and minor scales acapella using a high-quality pitch matching app for accuracy.

This may seem complicated for some people, and that's the difficulty with voice. We've heard people say, "How hard can singing really be?" The fact of the matter is that the voice is very complicated, and you've started your learning journey by purchasing and using this book. We've found that you can never complete your musical-learning journey. You may reach milestones along the way, but there's no destination in musical studies. It's the journey that matters.

A FINAL WORD

We are so grateful that you picked up our book, and we sincerely hope it has helped you along your journey. Believe in yourself. Work out at least five days a week using effective exercises. And remember to check out our website for free resources to support you on your singing path.

And as we always say, Rock On!

GLOSSARY

Belting: Belting is when a singer brings their chest voice higher than it would naturally go in their range, typically resulting in a louder, more powerful sound. The term originally comes from musical theater, where performers needed to project their voices to reach the back of the theater without amplification. Belting is often used in contemporary styles of music like pop, rock, and musical theater to convey emotional intensity. When done properly, belting can give a powerful, resonant, and emotionally charged quality to the voice.

Break: This is also referred to as the passaggio where a singer shifts from one register to another, or from one muscle group to another. It is the range of notes between speaking voice and higher singing voice. The break is the point of greatest perceived muscular tension and coordination between the muscle groups that control singing. If not managed carefully, this transition can lead to a noticeable change in the quality or volume of the voice, and it may sound like a voice flip or crack.

Chest voice: Chest voice is a type of vocal production that is typically associated with lower pitches and a fuller, richer sound. The term chest voice is used because the singer often feels vibrations in the chest when using this vocal register, thus giving the sensation as though the voice is resonating from that area. It is associated with the vocal register used for normal speech, and is often contrasted with head voice. Chest voice is created by shortening the vocal folds (vocal cords). The vocal folds vibrate more fully and at a slower rate compared to when singing in head voice.

Chromatic scale: In music, a chromatic scale is a scale that includes all twelve pitches within an octave. These pitches are a half step apart from one another. To give you an example, if you were to play a chromatic scale on a piano starting from middle C, you would play all the white and black keys in order until you reach the next C. So, the notes would be C, C♯, D, D♯, E, F, F♯, G, G♯, A, A♯, B, C.

CT muscle group: The CT or cricothyroid muscle is in the neck and is part of the larynx. The cricothyroid muscle works to stretch and thin the vocal folds, which increases their tension and results in the production of higher pitched sounds. It plays a crucial role in vocal register transition, especially when moving from the chest voice to the head voice or falsetto.

Diatonic Scale: The diatonic scale refers to a seven-note scale that includes five whole steps (whole tones) and two half steps (semitones) in each octave. The half steps are separated from each other by either two or three whole steps, depending on the specific type of diatonic scale. The most commonly recognized diatonic scales are the major and minor scales. For example, the C Major scale (C, D, E, F, G, A, B, C) is a type of diatonic scale. Here, the half steps are between E and F, and B and C, with whole steps between all the other notes.

Full step: A full step, also known as a whole step or a tone, is a musical interval in western music that is equivalent to two half steps or semitones. On a piano, a whole step would be the distance from one key to another with one black or white key in between.

Half step: A half step, also known as a semitone, is the smallest interval in western music. It refers to the distance between one note and the very next note up or down in pitch, whether it's on a piano keyboard, a guitar fretboard, or any other pitched instrument. On a piano, a half step would be the distance from one key to an adjacent black or white key whichever is closest.

Head voice: Head voice is a particular resonance or placement of the voice. It is typically associated with higher pitches and a lighter sound compared to chest voice (lower pitches). The term head voice is used because the sound resonates primarily in the areas around the upper part of the face, often felt as vibration or resonance in the head. Head voice often involves more elongation and thinning of the vocal folds (vocal cords), which is facilitated by the cricothyroid muscles (CT) in the larynx.

Intervals: An interval refers to the difference or distance in pitch between two notes. Intervals can be measured in terms of their size (the number of half steps or whole steps between the two notes) and their quality (whether they are major, minor, perfect, augmented, or diminished).

Key: A song key in music to the group of pitches, or scale, that form the basis of a music composition. The key of a song determines the tonic note or chord which is the home base or resolution point of the song and dictates the notes and chords that sound the best in that key. It also establishes the overall tonality (major or minor) of the piece, which significantly influences the song's mood or emotional tone. There are two main types of keys (but there are others): 1) major key which is often perceived as happy or bright; 2) minor key which is often perceived as sad, dark, or mysterious.

Lip trills/rolls: Lip trills, also known as lip rolls, lip bubbles, or lip buzzes, are the go-to vocal warm-up exercise used by singers. They are intended to help relax and warmup the muscles used for singing and to improve breath control. Singers can use lip trills to train for difficult passages in songs. To perform a lip trill, you generally follow these steps: 1) Relax your lips and face. The more relaxed your lips, the easier it will be to perform the trill. 2) Take a deep breath and exhale slowly, allowing your lips to vibrate or "trill" as you exhale. It should create a "brr" sound, like the sound a child may make when imitating how a motor sounds or some people may think of the sound as raspberries. 3) While maintaining this lip vibration, try to produce pitch by singing a note. Most singers usually sing a scale or a simple melody while doing the lip trill.

Mixed voice: Mixed voice refers to a blend or balance between chest voice and head voice. It is a technique where singers mix the resonance of chest voice and head voice to create a unified, blended sound across their vocal range.

Octave: In terms of musical notes, an octave refers to the distance between two notes that are seven diatonic (major or minor scale) steps apart. An octave is the interval between one musical pitch and another with double (or half) its frequency. In simple terms, it is the same note either sung higher or lower. For example, the distance from a C to the next C up or down on a keyboard is an octave.

Passaggio: See break.

Pentatonic scale: A pentatonic scale is a musical scale that consists of five notes per octave, in contrast to the seven-note scales such as the major or minor scales. There are several types of pentatonic scales, but the two most common ones are the major pentatonic scale and the minor pentatonic scale.

Range: This is all of the notes a vocalist can sing from lowest to highest.

Scale: Notes that are played one after another that follow a set pattern of intevals.

Singing vowels: Singing vowels refer to the specific ways in which singers shape their mouth, throat, and tongue to produce different vowel sounds. For example, ah as in father or oh as in go. Singing vowels that put more that one vowel sound together are called dipthongs. For example, boy (b-oh-yee).

TA muscle group: The TA, or thyroarytenoid muscle, is located within the larynx and forms the bulk of the vocal folds, often referred to as vocal cords. The thyroarytenoid muscle is primarily responsible for controlling the tension of the vocal folds. When this muscle contracts, it shortens and thickens the vocal folds, reducing the tension. This action generally lowers the pitch of the sound produced. The TA muscle is most active when you're singing in your lower ranges.

Transpose: Transposing a musical piece refers to the process of shifting all its notes up or down in pitch by a consistent interval. In other words, the entire melody, harmonies, and chord progressions of the song are moved to a different key while maintaining the same structural relationships between the notes. This is critical for the singer/vocalist as transposing a song will allow singers with different ranges to sing the same song.

Vocal break: See break.

Vocal folds: The vocal folds, also known as vocal cords, are a pair of soft tissue bands located in the larynx, or voice box, in the throat. They play a crucial role in the production of speech and singing. When we're not speaking or singing, the vocal folds remain open to allow for breathing. When we speak or sing, the vocal folds close to a specific spot and they tense. Each note you sing is a different configuration of muscles, tension and position. As air from the lungs is pushed out by the diaphragm, it causes the vocal folds to vibrate, producing sound. The pitch of the sound is determined by the tension and length of the vocal folds.

Warmup: Warming up is the process of preparing the voice for singing. Just like athletes need to warmup their muscles before exercising or playing a sport, singers need to warmup their vocal cords and associated muscles to prevent strain or injury and to get the best performance. In our studio, the foundation of our warmups are lip trills. A good warmup routine takes time and should not be rushed and is important for vocal health.

ACKNOWLEDGEMENTS

We set out to write a book that would competently answer the questions that we had as students, teachers, researchers, and performing artists. Along this path, we found both harmony and dissonance, joy and frustration – all a part of growing and learning the real value of the creative spirit. We've been honored to have encountered many fellow travelers on the musical path whose contributions have been pivotal, instrumental, and often unsung.

We want to thank our diligent and ever-curious students, who constantly challenge us with their questions and inspire us with their enthusiasm. They are the catalysts that drive us to dig deeper and aim higher. Their inquisitive natures remind us of the profound wonders of the human voice, and the need to delve into both the science and artistry of it in a way that satisfies their curiosity.

We want to thank those members of our studio who served as a living laboratory, who generously donated their time, shared their voices, and occasionally, their vulnerabilities – this work stands on the bedrock of your contributions. Your participation and patience ensured that the findings in this book are rooted in genuine human experiences.

We owe immeasurable debt to our professors of music and teachers through the decades who may have not had formal conservatory or university training, yet constantly worked to find the optimal path for each individual voice – it is this drive that led us to write this book. Your expertise, mentorship, and, above all, your unwavering faith in our music and this project have been our guiding stars. You've not only instilled in us the principles of rigorous scientific inquiry but also the art of storytelling that science often lacks but desperately needs.

We are grateful to our fellow musicians with whom we perform and collaborate – the maestros and the beginners alike. Thank you for being the soulful testament to the wonders of the voice. Their talent, heart, and insights were invaluable in adding nuance to this intricate tapestry of knowledge. They've shown, time and again, that the voice is not just about waves and frequencies, but about emotions, stories, and connections, and above all, expressions of individual artistry. Regardless of your technical musical level, we are all students who are striving to perfect our individual art.

Lastly, many thanks to our community partners and associates who believe in the commercial and societal potential of this venture. Their insights, expertise, and resources have been pivotal in bringing this book to the hands and voices of many.

This book, while written by two musicians, teachers, artists and researchers, is the fruit of many. To all who have been a part of this journey, directly or indirectly, we extend our deepest gratitude. Your voices echo on every page.